OLSAT™

GRADE 6 • GRADE 7 • GRADE 8

TEST PREP

OLSAT®
GRADE 6 • GRADE 7 • GRADE 8
TEST PREP
Level F

Gateway Gifted Resources™
www.GatewayGifted.com

PLEASE LEAVE US A REVIEW!

Thank you for selecting this book. We are a family-owned publishing company - a consortium of educators, book designers, illustrators, parents, and kid-testers.

We would be thrilled if you left us a quick review on the website where you purchased this book!

The Gateway Gifted Resources™ Team
www.GatewayGifted.com

TABLE OF CONTENTS

INTRODUCTION

ABOUT THIS BOOK: This book helps prepare kids for the OLSAT® Level F, a test given to sixth through eighth graders. Not only will this publication help prepare kids for the OLSAT®, these logic-based exercises may also be used for other gifted test preparation and as critical thinking exercises. This book has four parts.

1. **Introduction:** About this book & the OLSAT®, Test-Taking Tips, Points Tracking, and Question Examples

2. **Practice Test 1 (Workbook Format):** These pages are designed similarly to content tested in the OLSAT®'s 15 test question types. Questions are grouped by question type, so that your student can more easily comprehend question material.

Unless your student already has experience with OLSAT® prep materials, you should complete Practice Test 1 (Workbook Format) together with no time limit. **Before doing this section with your student, read the Question Examples & Explanations.**

3. **Practice Test 2 & Practice Test 3:** These help kids develop critical thinking and test-taking skills. It provides an introduction to standardized testing in a relaxed manner (parents provide guidance if needed) and an opportunity for kids to focus on a group of questions for a longer time period. This part is also a way for parents to identify points of strength/ challenges.

Questions in Practice Test 2 & 3 are not grouped by question type. When your student takes the test, questions will most likely not be grouped by question type.

4. **Answer Keys:** This has the answers to Practice Test 1, 2, and 3 as well as brief answer explanations.

ABOUT THE OLSAT® LEVEL F

- The OLSAT® Level F is given to middle schoolers.
- It has 72 questions in multiple choice format.
- The test lasts approximately one hour.
- Schools use the test for admittance to gifted/advanced programs.
- Questions are different than those found on typical grade level quizzes, tests, and standardized testing.
- Here are the three OLSAT® Level F question types and corresponding question sections:

  -Verbal: Antonyms, Sentence Completion, Sentence Arrangement, Arithmetic Reasoning, Verbal Analogies, Verbal Classification, Logical Selection, Word/Letter Matrix, and Inferences

  -Non Verbal: Figure Analogies, Figure Series, Pattern Matrix

  -Quantitative: Numeric Inferences, Numeric Matrix, Numeric Series

ABOUT OLSAT® TESTING PROCEDURES: These vary by school. Tests may be given individually or in a group. These tests may be used as the single factor for admission to gifted programs, or they may be used in combination with IQ tests or as part of a student "portfolio." They are used by some schools together with tests like Iowa Assessments™. Check with your testing site to determine its specific testing procedures.

QUESTION NOTE: Because each student has different cognitive abilities, the questions in this book are at varied skill levels. The exercises may or may not require a great deal of parental guidance to complete, depending on your student's abilities, prior test prep experience, or prior testing experience. Most sections of Practice Test 1 begin with a relatively easy question. We suggest always completing at least the first question together, ensuring your student is not confused about what the question asks or with the directions.

SCORING NOTE: Check with your school for its scoring procedure and admissions requirements. Here is a general summary of the OLSAT® scoring process. First, your child's raw score is established. This is the number of questions correctly answered. Points are not deducted for questions answered incorrectly. Next, this score is compared to other test-takers of his/her same age group to then calculate the percentile rank. If your student achieved the percentile rank of 98%, then (s)he scored as well as or better than 98% of test-takers. Note that a percentile rank "score" cannot be obtained from our practice material. This material has not been given to a large enough sample of test-takers to develop any kind of base score necessary for percentile rank calculations.

TEST-TAKING TIPS

• **Be sure your student looks carefully at each answer choice.** OLSAT® questions can be quite challenging. Even if your student thinks (s)he knows the answer - (s)he should look at each choice.

• **Test-takers receive points for the number of correct answers.** If your student says that (s)he does not know the answer, (s)he should first eliminate answers that are clearly incorrect. Guess instead of leaving a question blank.

• **In Practice Test 1, go through the exercises together by talking about them:** what the exercise is asking them to do and what makes the answer choices correct/incorrect. This will familiarize your student with working through exercises and will help to develop a process of elimination (getting rid of incorrect answer choices).

• **Remember common sense tips like getting enough sleep.** It has been scientifically proven that kids perform below their grade level when tired. **Provide a breakfast for sustained energy and concentration** (complex carbohydrates and protein; avoid foods/drinks high in sugar). Have them use the restroom prior to the test.

POINTS TRACKING

To increase engagement and to add an incentive to complete book exercises, a game theme accompanies this book. As your student completes the three Practice Tests, (s)he earns 1 point per page. After completing all pages, they will have earned 68 points. Some parents may want to offer a special incentive as well for completion, although this is at the parent's discretion.

A CHALLENGE FOR YOU!

We've got a challenge for you! Are you up for it?

This book is filled with mind-bending, challenging questions.

For every page you do, you earn 1 point.

Do you think you can finish the book?
Use the space below to track your points.

The questions start on page 6.

Remember to:

- pay close attention to each word (or number) in the question
- look carefully at all choices before choosing an answer
- keep trying even if some questions are hard

CAN YOU EARN 68 POINTS?

POINTS TRACKING

Date	Points	Date	Points	Date	Points
_____	_____	_____	_____	_____	_____
_____	_____	_____	_____	_____	_____

QUESTION EXAMPLES & EXPLANATIONS

This section introduces the 15 question types on the OLSAT® Level F using basic examples and explanations.

VERBAL SECTION

1. Antonyms
Directions: Read the sentence and choose which word is the opposite of the word in quotation marks.

The opposite of "best" is _____.

A. slow   B. bad   C. worst   D. great

The opposite of "best" is "worst." This section tests a student's vocabulary and their ability to reason and recognize a word's true opposite. In the example above, some students may choose "bad," when "worst" is actually the true opposite. Be sure to carefully go through the choices to pick the true opposite.

2. Sentence Completion
Directions: Read the sentence. There is a missing word. Which answer choice goes best in the sentence?

If you are not _____ with the vase, it will break.

A. careless   B. careful   C. clear   D. risky

The answer is B. Here, be sure to pay attention to each word in the sentence. After choosing your answer, reread the sentence together with your answer choice. Pay attention for "negative" words like "not." Also pay attention for "contrasting" words like "however," "but," "despite," that can be used to show contrasting ideas in sentences.

3. Sentence Arrangement
Directions: The words below need to be arranged to make the best sentence. Which letter would the first word of the sentence begin with? Here are the words:

yummy   for   waited   puppies   a   treat   the   two

A. P   B. T   C. W   D. Y

The correct sentence is: The two puppies waited for a yummy treat. The answer is B. Here are some tips.

1- Finding the main subject and verb will help you establish the basic structure. First, identify the verb(s). This will give you a clue to the subject. Then, try to identify the subject. Some sentences will have more than one noun that could be the subject. If there is more than one noun, test each one.
2- Group related words: Identify phrases or groups of words that belong together (e.g., adjectives with nouns, adverbs with verbs). This can help you see how parts of the sentence connect.
3- Look for clues: Some sentences may have words that indicate time (e.g., "yesterday," "now"), conjunctions (e.g., "and," "but"), or prepositions (e.g., "in," "on") that provide context and help you organize the sentence.

4. Arithmetic Reasoning   Directions: Read the question then choose your answer.

Julia and Mike had pizza for lunch. Julia ate 7 slices. Mark ate 2 more slices than Julia. How many slices did they eat all together?

A. 9   B. 7   C. 16   D. 12

First, find the number Mark ate. He ate 2 more than Julia, so 2 + 7 = 9. Mark at 9 slices. Julia ate 7 slices. So, 9+7 = 16. These questions are not a test solely of math abilities. They are an assessment of your student's ability to read word problems, turn the words into equations, and solve the equations.

5. Logical Selection
Directions: Read the sentence and choose which word best completes the sentence.

A lake must have _____.

A. boats   B. fish   C. swimmers   D. water

The answer is water. Here, you need to use logic and reasoning to figure out which choice is the only one that is truly needed.

6. Verbal Analogies
Directions: Look at the first set of words. Try to figure out how they belong together. Next, look at the second set of words. The answer is missing. Figure out which answer choice would make the second set go together in the same way that the first set goes together.

toe > foot : petal > ?   A. stem   B. bee   C. leg   D. flower

The answer is D. Here are some strategies to help arrive at the correct answer:
• Try to come up with a "rule" describing how the first set goes together. Take this rule, apply it to the first word in the second set. Which answer choice makes the second set follow the same "rule?" If more than one choice works, you need a more specific rule. Here, a "rule" for the first set is that "the first word (toe) is part of the second word (foot)." In the next set, using this rule, "flower" is the answer. A petal is part of a flower.
• Another strategy is to come up with a sentence describing how the first set of words go together. A sentence would be: A toe is part of a foot. Then, take this sentence and apply it to the word in the second set: A petal is part of a ? Figure out which answer choice would best complete the sentence. (It would be "flower.")
• Do not choose a word simply because it has to do with the first set. For example, choice A ("stem") has to do with a petal, but does not follow the rule.

Here are more simple examples. Read the "Question" then "Answer Choices" to your student. Which choice goes best? (The answer is underlined.)

Analogy Logic	Question	Answer Choices (Answer is Underlined)			
• Antonyms	On is to Off -as- Hot is to ?	Warm	Sun	Cold	Oven
• Synonyms	Big is to Large -as- Horrible is to ?	Tired	Stale	Sour	Awful
• Whole: Part	Tree is to Branch -as- House is to ?	Street	Apartment	Room	Home
• Degree	Good is to Excellent -as- Tired is to ?	Boring	Exhausted	Drowsy	Slow
• Object: Location	Sun is to Sky -as- Swing is to ?	Playground	Monkey Bars	Sidewalk	Grass
• Object: Creator	Painting is to Artist -as- Furniture is to ?	Carpenter	Tool	Chair	Potter
• Object: Container	Ice Cube is to Ice Tray -as- Flower is to ?	Petal	Vase	Smell	Florist
• Object: 3D Shape	Ball is to Sphere -as- Dice is to ?	Line	Square	Cone	Cube
• Object: Location Used	Jet is to Sky -as- Canoe is to ?	Boat	Paddle	Water	Sail

7. Verbal Classification
Directions: These words all go together in a certain way except for one. Which word does not go with the others?

A. fork   B. chopsticks   C. knife   D. meat   E. spoon

Here, D is the answer. All the others are utensils used for eating. However, meat is a kind of food. Even though meat has to do with food, it is not like the others.

Try to come up with a "rule" describing how the words are alike, except for one. If more than one choice does not follow the rule, then try a more specific rule. More examples are on the next page.

Read the list of 5 words to your student, then ask which does not belong.
The gray text lists the question's logic. The underlined text is the word that does not belong.

- functions and uses of common objects (i.e., writing and drawing / measuring / cutting / drinking / eating)
Fork / Chopsticks / Knife / <u>Meat</u> / Spoon   (Utensils Used For Eating)

- location of common objects
Refrigerator / <u>Shower</u> / Cabinet / Table / Oven   (Found In Kitchens)

- appearance of common objects (i.e., color; objects in pairs; objects with stripes vs. spots; object's shape)
<u>Box</u> / Baseball / Sphere / Basketball / Globe   (Round)

- characteristics of common objects (i.e., hot, cold)
Ice / Igloo / Popsicle / <u>Coffee</u> / Snowman   (Cold Things)

- animal/human homes
Aquarium / <u>Fish</u> / Barn / Nest / Beehive   (Animal Homes)

- animal types
Leopard / Cheetah / Lion / Tiger / <u>Monkey</u>   (Cats)

- natural habitats
Swamp / River / <u>Mountain</u> / Ocean / Pond   (Water)

- food types
Cake / Bread / Donut / <u>Syrup</u> / Cookie   (Baked Foods)

- food growing location (i.e., on a tree, under the ground as a root, or on a vine)
<u>Melon</u> / Potato / Carrot / Onion / Radish   (Root Vegetables)

- professions, community helpers
Doctor / Teacher / <u>Wizard</u> / Fireman / Vet   (Community Helpers)

- clothing (i.e., in what weather it's worn; on what body part it's worn)
Crown / Cowboy Hat / Cap / <u>Gloves</u> / Helmet   (Worn On Head)

- transportation (i.e., where things travel, land/water/air; do they have wheels?)
Cruise Ship / Canoe / <u>Car</u> / Yacht / Kayak   (Travel On Water)

8. Letter Matrix / Word Matrix

Directions: Look at what is in the box. You will see either words or simply letters. They go together in a certain way. Then, look at the answer choices. What answer choice would go where the question mark is?

e e	t r	t r e e
l l	c a	?

A. call   B. cart   C. trace   D. eel

Here, take the 2 letters in the second set of letters "tr" and put them in front of the 2 letters in the first set "ee": tr + ee = tree. With the bottom row, do the same: ca + ll = call. Therefore, choice A is the answer.

Note that some questions will have words (not letters). An example in Practice Test 1 includes words, for your reference. With these types of questions (questions that include words), the pattern involves words that are in alphabetical order or words that are opposites.

9. Inferences

Directions: Read the sentences. Based on the information given in the sentences, choose the correct answer choice.

Ana runs faster than Mia. Mia runs faster than Lily. Which one is true?

A   Ana runs slower than Lily.

B   Mia runs faster than Ana.

C   Lily runs faster than Ana.

D   Ana runs faster than Lily.

E   Lily and Mia run at the same speed.

In this simple example, carefully follow the logic given in the statements. First statement: "Ana runs faster than Mia." This means Ana is faster than Mia (A > M). Second statement: "Mia runs faster than Lily." This means Mia is faster than Lily (M > L). Combine the two pieces of information. Ana is faster than Mia, and Mia is faster than Lily (A > M > L). Therefore, Ana must also be faster than Lily, because Ana is the fastest of all three. Next, carefully read each answer choice to find which one matches the information you just evaluated. The only answer choice that is true is choice D, "Ana runs faster than Lily."

NON-VERBAL SECTION
10. Figure Analogies

Directions: The pictures inside the top boxes go together in a certain way. Which answer choice goes with the picture in the bottom box like the pictures in the top boxes do? (The word "picture" here refers to a "figure" that can consist of shapes, lines, etc.)

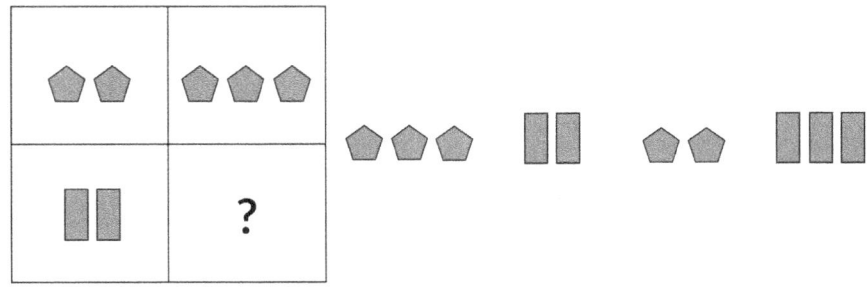

Explanation Come up with a "rule" describing how the top set is related. This shows how the left box "changes" into the right box. On the left are 2 pentagons. On the right are 3 pentagons. The rule/change is that one more of the same kind of shape was added. On the bottom are 2 rectangles. The first choice is incorrect because it shows 3 pentagons - not the same shapes as the bottom box. The second choice is incorrect - it only shows 2 rectangles. The third choice is incorrect - it has 2 pentagons. The last choice is correct - there are 3 rectangles (1 more of the same shapes that were in the left box).

Here are 12 <u>basic</u> Figure Analogy "changes."

1. Color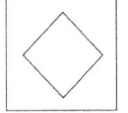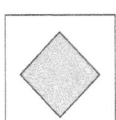

2. Size

3. Amount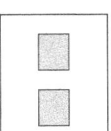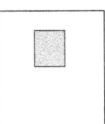

4. Color Reversal

5. Whole to Part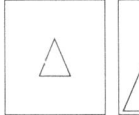

6. Shape Sides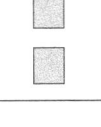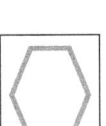

The list continues on the next page.

7. Rotation: 90° clockwise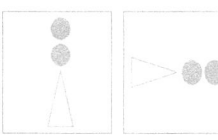

8. Rotation: 90° counter-clockwise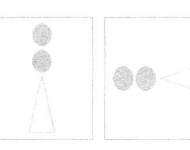

9. Line Direction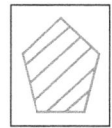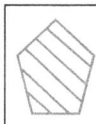

10. Flip/ Mirror Image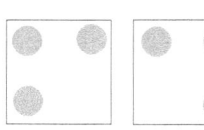

11. Two Changes: Rotation & Quantity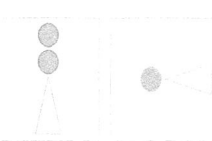

12. Two Changes: Rotation & Color

11. Pattern Matrices

Directions: Look at the pictures inside the boxes. They make a pattern. Look at the last box. It is empty. Look next to the boxes at the row of pictures. Which one should go inside the empty box in the bottom row?

Explanation Across the top row, here is the pattern: 2 shapes - 1 shape - 2 shapes (the same kind of shape). The middle row has this pattern also. In the bottom row, we see 2 shapes - 1 shape -

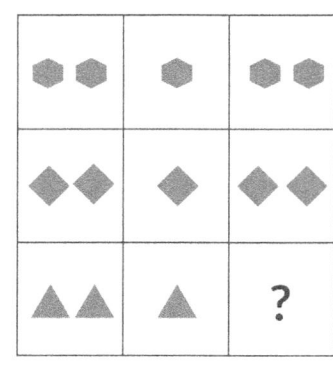  

and... what would be the answer? It would be 2 shapes of the same kind of shape (triangles). The answer is D.

Common logic themes found in Figure Analogies are also found in Pattern Matrices.

12. Figure Series

Directions: In this row of boxes, the pictures belong together in some way. Another picture should go inside the empty box. Which picture in the row of answer choices should go in this empty box?

Explanation Here, figure out the pattern inside the boxes. First, the star is on the right side of the triangle, then it moves to the bottom of the triangle, then to the left side, and then to the right side. Where would the star move next? It would move to the bottom, Choice C. (The star moves clockwise around the triangle's sides.)

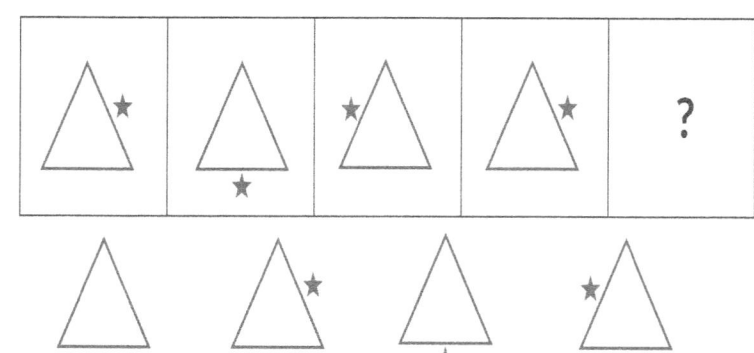

Common logic found in Figure Analogies is also found in Figure Series questions.

QUANTITATIVE SECTION

13. Numeric Matrix

Directions: Look at the numbers inside the boxes. They go together in a certain way. Which answer choice would go inside the empty box in the bottom row?

2	3	4
7	8	9
12	13	?

A 14   B 15   C 18   D 11

Here, try to come up with a "rule" that applies to the numbers going across the rows. There is also a "rule" that applies going down the columns.

Going across the rows, you see that the "rule" is "add 1."
Going down the columns, you see that the "rule" is "add 5."

Given this, the answer is A.

14. Numeric Inferences

Directions: Look at the first two sets of numbers. Come up with a rule that both of these sets follow. Take this rule to figure out which answer choice goes in the place of the question mark.

[10 →5]   [8 →4]   [14 →?]   A.2   B.7   C.28   D.16   E.1

Come up with a rule to explain how the first number "changes" into the second. It could use addition, subtraction, multiplication, or division. Write the rule by each pair. Make sure it works with both pairs. The rule is "÷ by 2," so 7 is the answer.

15. Numeric Series

Directions: Which answer choice would continue the pattern?

15   13   11   9   7   ?   A.1   B.3   C.5   D.6   E.4

The numbers make a pattern. To help figure out the pattern, notice the difference between each number and the next. In this basic example, the pattern is: -2.

In easier questions, the difference between all consecutive numbers is the same (i.e., the difference between 15 & 13 = 2 and between 13 & 11 = 2). However, sometimes the difference will not continuously repeat itself, as in these examples:

9	8	6	5	3	2	?	The pattern is: -1, -2, -1, -2, etc. & the answer is 0.
1	2	4	7	11	16	?	The pattern is: +1, +2, +3, +4, etc. & the answer is 22.
4	5	9	4	5	9	?	The pattern is: 4-5-9 & the answer is 4.
0	10	0	20	0	30	?	Note: this pattern "skips." Every other number is 0. Also, every other number between a "0" has a pattern of +10 The answer is 0.

-Practice Test 1 (Workbook Format) Begins On The Next Page.-

ANTONYMS

Directions: Read the sentence and choose which answer is the opposite of the word given.

Example

The opposite of silent is _____.

    Ⓐ calm   Ⓑ bright   Ⓒ noisy   Ⓓ rapid   Ⓔ tranquil

1   **The opposite of reject is _____.**

    Ⓐ dismiss   Ⓑ deny   Ⓒ prepare   Ⓓ accept   Ⓔ consider

2   **The opposite of elevate is _____.**

    Ⓐ ascend   Ⓑ hoist   Ⓒ lower   Ⓓ stabilize   Ⓔ uplift

3   **The opposite of import is _____.**

    Ⓐ export   Ⓑ report   Ⓒ transport   Ⓓ receive   Ⓔ acquire

4   **The opposite of reluctantly is _____.**

    Ⓐ unwillingly   Ⓑ ethically   Ⓒ cautiously   Ⓓ occasionally   Ⓔ eagerly

SENTENCE COMPLETION

Directions: Read the sentence. There is a missing word. Look at the row of answer choices below the sentence. Which word would go best in the sentence?

Example

The garbage has become _____ after sitting in the sun all day. Get rid of it immediately!

  A rancid   *B* pleasant   *C* cleaner   *D* enlarged   *E* inflated

5   **The natural beauty of the landscape is an important _____ for attracting tourists.**

     A obstacle   *B* asset   *C* flaw   *D* barrier   *E* festivity

6   **To achieve the best performance, you must find the _____ settings for your computer.**

     A random   *B* irregular   *C* optimal   *D* erratic   *E* uncommon

7   **The coach held extra practices to _____ the talents of the aspiring athletes.**

     A cultivate   *B* compete   *C* diminish   *D* recede   *E* exhaust

8   **The Sahara Desert spans a large portion of North Africa, but it is _____ uninhabited due to the _____ conditions.**

     A densely, mild   *B* scarcely, harsh   *C* heavily, favorable   *D* quite, temperate   *E* fully, parched

SENTENCE ARRANGEMENT

Note: Be sure to pay attention to whether you are asked to find the <u>first</u> word of the sentence or the <u>last</u> word of the sentence.

Example

Directions: The words below need to be arranged to make the best sentence. Which letter would the <u>first</u> word of the sentence begin with? Here are the words:

believe	you	in	should	always	yourself
A F	B B	C I	D Y	E S	

9   The words below need to be arranged to make the best sentence. Which letter would the <u>last</u> word of the sentence begin with? Here are the words:

everything	a	positive	better	makes	attitude
A A	B B	C P	D M	E E	

Example Answer: D: Correct sentence: You should always believe in yourself.
(The answers for the rest are in the Answer Key.)

10 The words below need to be arranged to make the best sentence.
Which letter would the last word of the sentence begin with?
Here are the words:

who   person   works   succeeds   hard   the

A T   B W   C P   D H   E S

11 The words below need to be arranged to make the best sentence.
Which letter would the last word of the sentence begin with?
Here are the words:

great   I   to   work   ready   start   and   feel

A G   B T   C I   D W   E R

12 The words below need to be arranged to make the best sentence.
Which letter would the last word of the sentence begin with?
Here are the words:

lunch   already   I   had   my   friends   with

A A   B L   C H   D F   E M

ARITHMETIC REASONING

Note: The primary skill tested here is <u>not</u> your student's math level. You'll find some questions use quite basic math operations. The primary skill tested here involves taking the words in the math problem, turning the words into the correct math equations, and solving the equations.

Directions: Read the question then choose your answer.

Example 1

Four friends went to buy apples. Mia bought 3 bags, James bought 2 bags, Olivia bought 5 bags, and Ethan bought 4 bags. If each bag contains 8 apples, how many apples did all four friends buy in total?

Ⓐ 22   Ⓑ 48   Ⓒ 72   Ⓓ 112   Ⓔ 120

Example 2

What number is thirty less than four times fifteen?

Ⓐ 45   Ⓑ 30   Ⓒ 55   Ⓓ 60   Ⓔ 75

Example Answers: 1. D. The total number of bags is: $3 + 2 + 5 + 4 = 14$. Each bag contains 8 apples. So, $8 \times 14 = 112$ apples.

2. B. "Thirty less than four times fifteen" can be written as: $(4 \times 15) - 30$.

13 What number is thirty-five less than five times eighteen?

A 60   B 90   C 35   D 45   E 55

14 Liam finished his Math test twenty-five minutes early. If Noah finished his Math test twenty minutes after Liam, how many minutes early did he finish the test?

A 5   B 10   C 15   D 20   E 30

15 Olivia spends half an hour walking to the library in the morning. She studies there for 5 hours and 30 minutes. Afterward, she spends 30 minutes walking to the coffee shop. In the evening, she walks half an hour to get home. How many total hours does Olivia spend each day walking and studying?

A 6   B 7   C 9   D 7.5   E 8

16 What number is twenty-three less than twenty-eight plus seventy-two?

A 75   B 77   C 72   D 80   E 82

LOGICAL SELECTION

Directions: Read the sentence and choose which word best completes the sentence.

Tip: Be sure to think carefully about whether or not each answer choice is truly needed.

Example

A sandwich must always have _____.

A bread   B cheese   C lettuce   D tomato   E meat

17   **A painting must always have _____.**

A a frame   B many colors   C a surface   D a signature   E a title

18   **A shoe must always have _____.**

A laces   B a sole   C leather   D a brand logo   E a tongue

19   **A pen must always have _____.**

A a cap   B a metal tip   C ink   D black ink   E plastic case

20   **A shirt must always have _____.**

A sleeves   B buttons   C a collar   D fabric   E pockets

VERBAL ANALOGIES

Directions: The first set of words goes together in a certain way. Look at the second set of words. The answer is missing. Which answer choice would make the second set go together in the same way that the first set goes together?

Tip: Think of a "rule" or a sentence describing how each pair goes together.

Example

enormous → large : freezing → ?

A snowy   B ice   C temperature   D cold   E arctic

21   **heavy → weight : fast → ?**

   A speed   B quick   C race   D engine   E vehicle

22   **movies → theater : artifacts → ?**

   A quarry   B museum   C archeologist   D university   E cemetery

23   **wagon → car : typewriter → ?**

   A printer   B calculator   C computer   D cell phone   E notebook

24   **lung → air : engine → ?**

   A vehicle   B exhaust   C water   D fuel   E heat

Example Answer: D. Enormous means very large. Freezing means very cold.

VERBAL CLASSIFICATION

Directions: Which word does not go with the others?

Tips: Figure out how all of the words, except for one, are alike.

Try to come up with a "rule" describing this. Then, take this "rule," and figure out which of the answer choices does not follow it.

If you find that more than one choice does not follow the rule, then try to come up with a rule that is more specific.

The "rule" in the example is: words that describe the position or orientation of lines.

A "point" is a location on a line. However, this word does not describe lines or the orientation of lines.

Example

1   **Which word does not go with the others?**

      Ⓐ vertical   Ⓑ perpendicular   Ⓒ diagonal   Ⓓ point   Ⓔ parallel

25 **Which word does not go with the others?**

A halt   B protect   C cease   D suspend   E discontinue

26 **Which word does not go with the others?**

A reporter   B surgeon   C pharmacist   D dentist   E nurse

27 **Which word does not go with the others?**

A sack   B suitcase   C satchel   D backpack   E carton

28 **Which word does not go with the others?**

A alliance   B partnership   C member   D coalition   E union

LETTER MATRIX / WORD MATRIX

Directions: Look at what is in the box. You will see either words or simply letters. They go together in a certain way. Then, look at the answer choices. What answer choice would go where the question mark is?

Tips: First, figure out if the things in the boxes are words or simply letters. Then, try to figure out how they go together. First, look across. Across the rows, the first word ends in "eal." The second word ends in "eat." The third word ends in "old." On the first row, the words start with "s." On the second row the words start with "m." Given these two patterns, we can see that "mold" is the answer.

In Example 2, across the rows, the words are in alphabetical order. (However, note in #31 that the words are in alphabetical order, but you must look up and down the columns.)

Finally, in questions like #29, #30, and #32, you must figure out the letter pattern that occurs as you go across the rows.

EXAMPLE 1

seal	seat	sold
meal	meat	?

A moms   B most   C told   D mold   E bold

EXAMPLE 2

arc	bacon	canned
xylophone	yacht	?

A design   B zinc   C window   D message   E saved

29

bet	**bat**	**beat**
bot	**bat**	**?**

A bait   B beam   C boad   D bead   E boat

30

me	**mt**	**meet**
ro	**rm**	**?**

A moon   B reel   C room   D rope   E rest

31

prime	**river**	**theory**
quest	**shore**	**?**

A universal   B prediction   C focus   D endeavor   E capable

32

start	**gent**	**stage**
realm	**chat**	**?**

A range   B leaf   C real   D reach   E role

INFERENCES

Directions: Read the sentences. Based on the information given in the sentences, choose the correct answer choice.

Tips:
Be sure to carefully read each sentence.

Pay attention to keywords like these:
- only
- if
- and
- or
- not

Use the given rules to analyze the facts. Then, determine which conditions are true or false based on the sentences in the question. Finally, review the choices and eliminate ones that don't follow the rules described in the sentences in the question.

EXAMPLE

Read the sentences and choose an answer.

Kevin will play soccer only if the weather is good. If Kevin is tired, he will not go to the gym. Kevin is at the gym and is playing soccer. Therefore:

A. Kevin is tired and the weather is bad.

B. Kevin is not tired and the gym is closed.

C. Kevin is not tired and the weather is bad.

D. Kevin is not tired and the weather is good.

E. Kevin is tired and the weather is good.

The sentence states that Kevin is playing soccer. If he is playing soccer, that means the weather must be good. The sentence also states that Kevin is at the gym. If Kevin is at the gym, he must not be tired. We know that he will not go to the gym if he is tired. Therefore, the correct answer is D: "Kevin is not tired and the weather is good."

33 Tia runs faster than Joe. Joe runs slower than Sam but faster than Adam. Which of the following is true?

 A Joe runs the fastest.

 B Joe runs the slowest.

 C Sam runs faster than Tia.

 D Adam runs the slowest.

 E Joe runs faster than Tia.

34 Lee has fewer books than Olivia. Olivia has more books than Ellie. Which of the following is true?

 A Ellie has the most books.

 B Ellie and Lee have the same number of books.

 C Olivia has the fewest books.

 D Lee has the most books.

 E Olivia has the most books.

35 Alex is older than Ben. Chris is younger than Dev. Emily is older than Ben but younger than Chris. Which of the following must be true?

 A Ben is the youngest.

 B Chris is the oldest.

 C Dev is the youngest.

 D Emily is older than Alex.

 E Chris is younger than Ben.

FIGURE ANALOGIES

Directions: Look at the top boxes. The pictures inside belong together in a certain way. Look at the bottom boxes. One is empty. Which answer choice would go with the picture in the bottom box in the same way that the top boxes go together?

Tips: Use the same methodology to complete Figure Analogies as you used for Verbal Analogies. Work through these together so your test-taker sees how the first set is related.

Together, come up with a "rule" to describe how the first set is related. Then, in the second set, look at the first picture. Take this "rule," use it together with the first picture, and figure out which of the answer choices would follow that same rule.

For answer choices that do not follow this rule, eliminate them. If your student finds that more than one choice follows this rule, then try to come up with a rule that is more specific.

In the example, the bottom shape flips/rotates 180°. Then, the two shapes come together. Also, the inner designs switch (vertical lines and black).

EXAMPLE

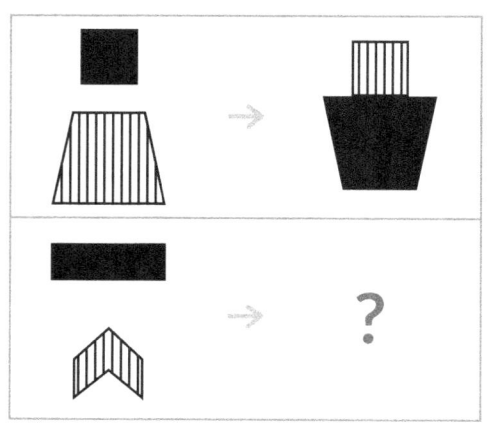

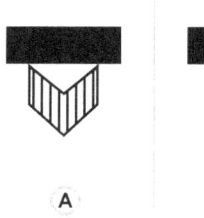 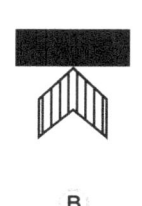 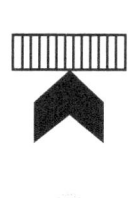  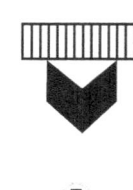

A   B   C   D   E

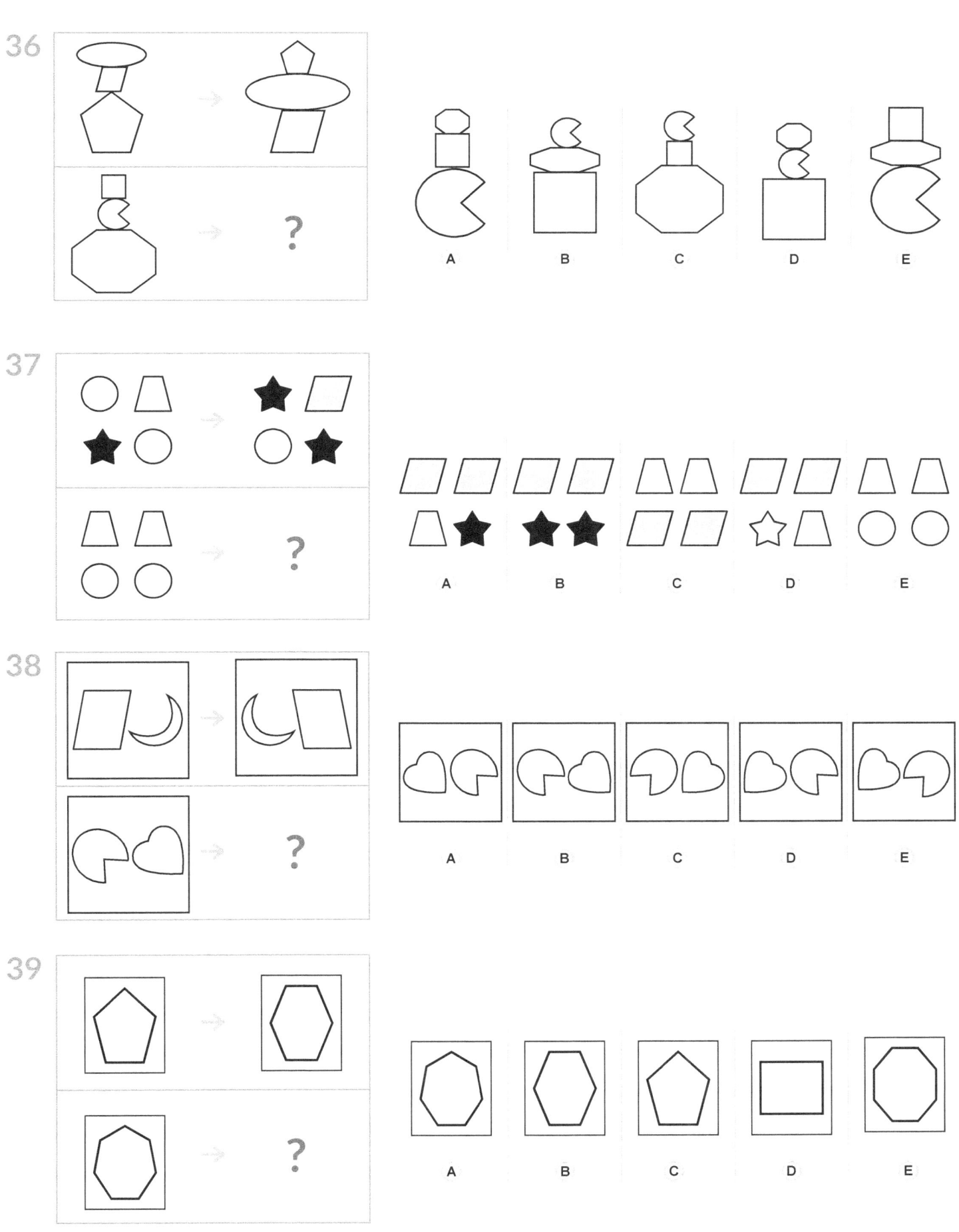

FIGURE SERIES

Directions: The pictures inside the boxes go together in a certain way. Another picture should go inside the empty box. Under the boxes is a row of pictures. Which one should go in this empty box?

Tips: See if you can spot the pattern that the design in each box has made, as you go from left to right.

The last box must continue this pattern.

In the example below, there are four shapes aligned vertically. As you move to the next box, you can see the top shape moves to the bottom of the shape group.

EXAMPLE

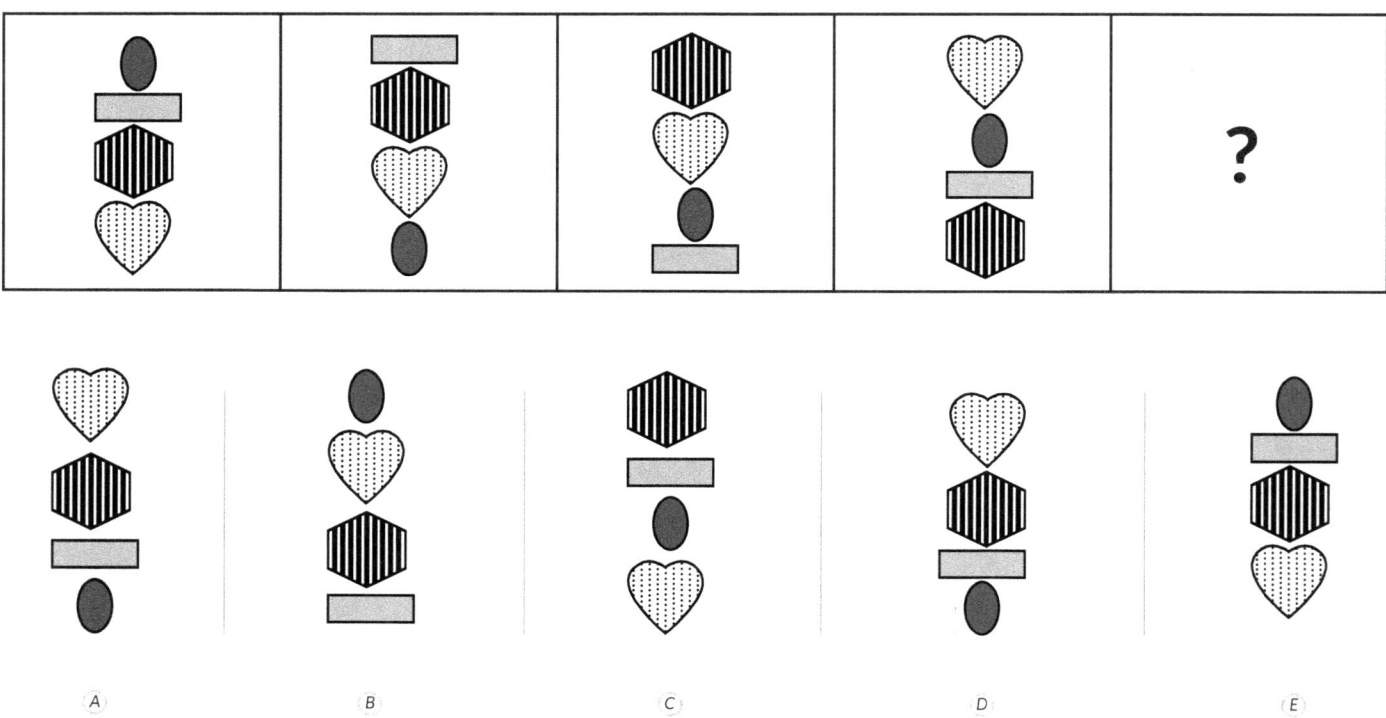

40

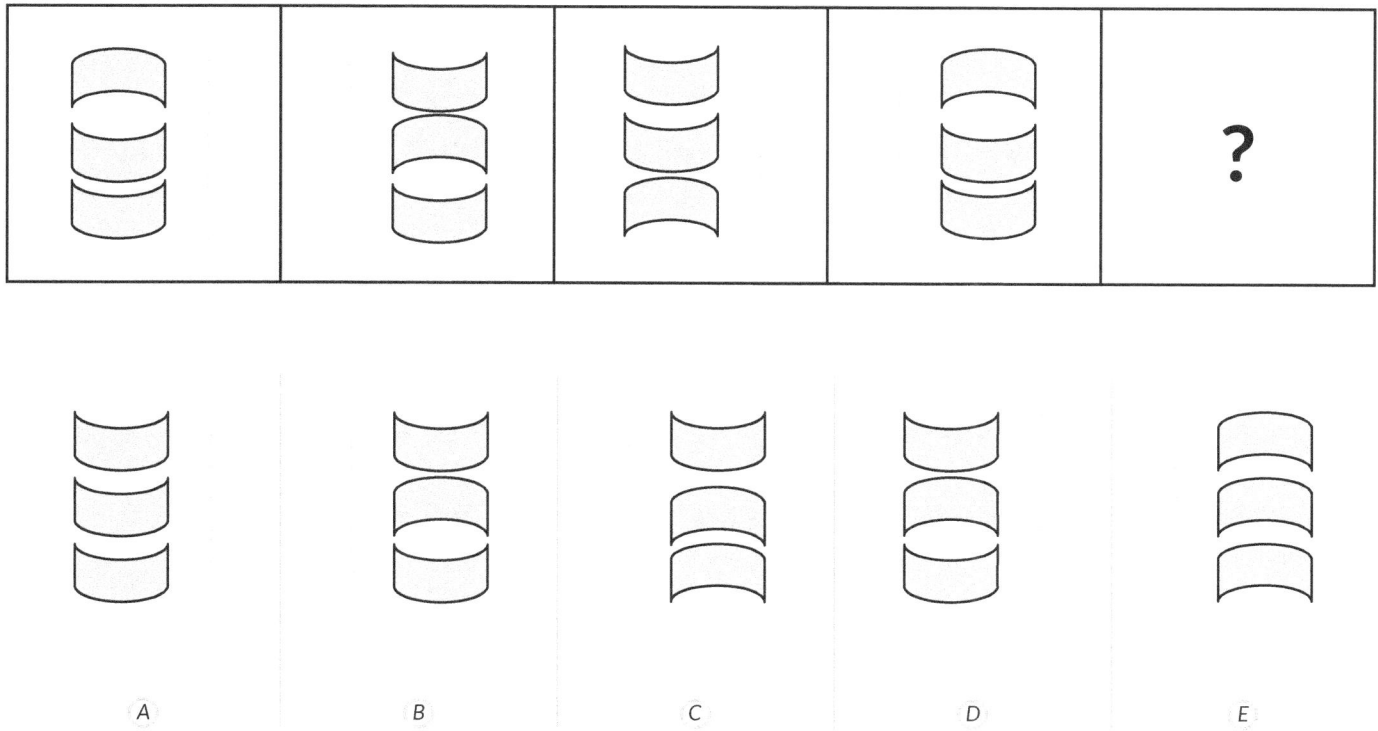

41

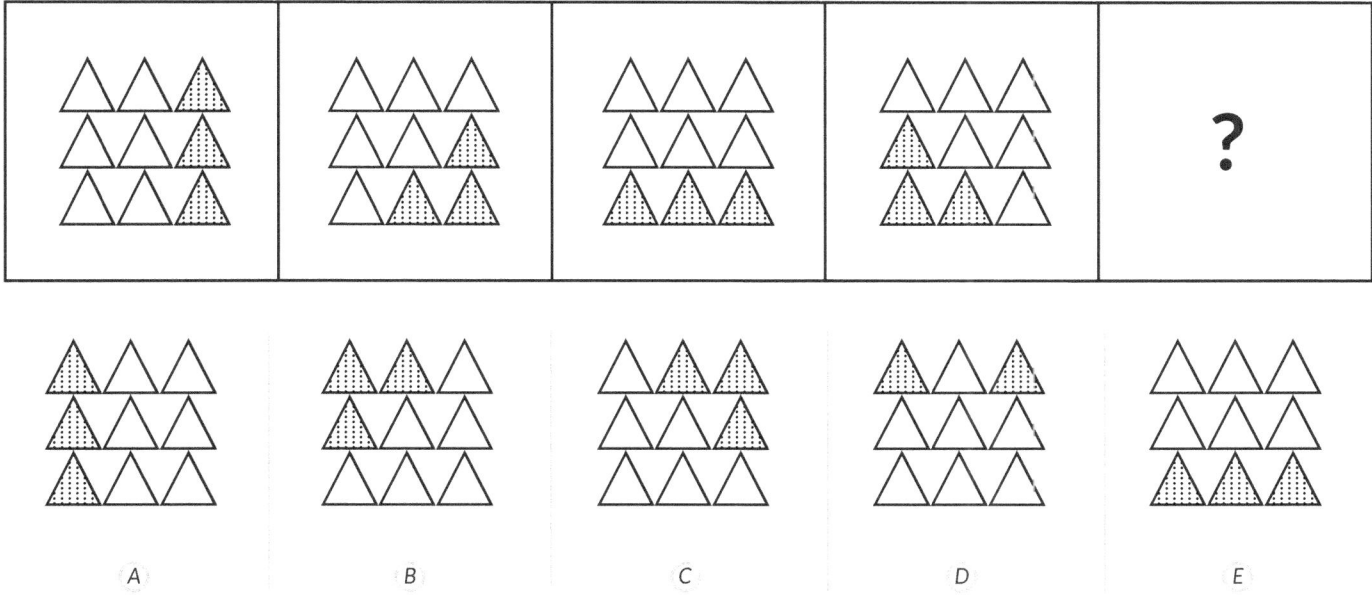

PATTERN MATRIX

Directions: Look at the pictures inside the boxes. They go together in a certain way. Which answer choice would go inside the empty box in the bottom row?

Tips: See if you can spot the pattern that the design in each box has made, as you go from left to right.

There may also be a pattern that goes up and down.

The last box must continue this pattern.

In the example below, going across the first row, we see that the gray bar decreases each time (and stays on same side of the box). The gray bar continues its decreasing pattern as you go across the rows.

EXAMPLE

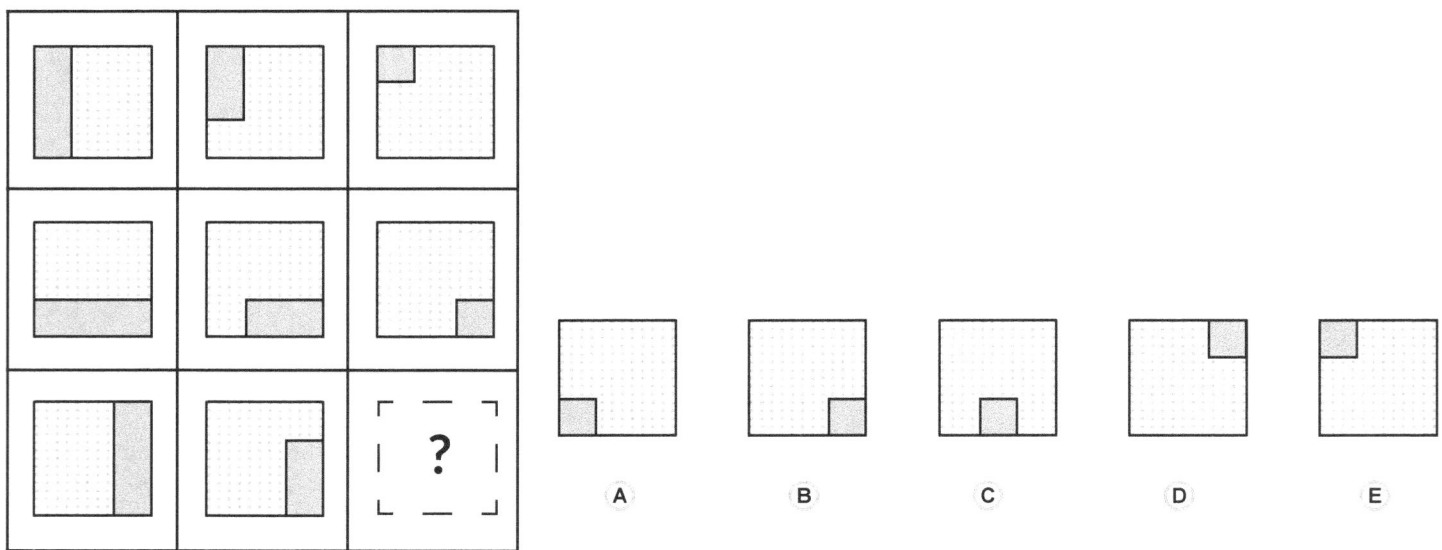

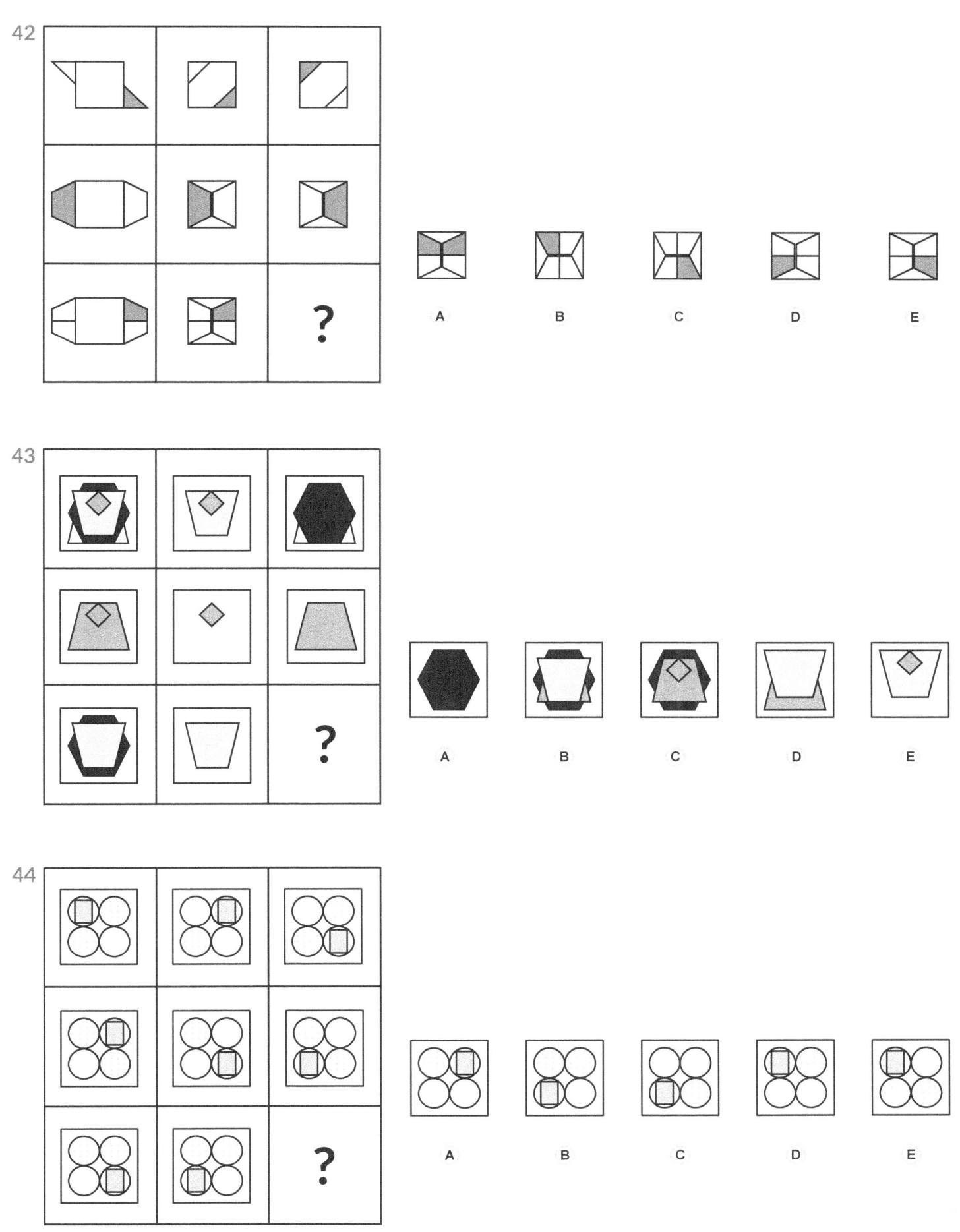

NUMERIC MATRIX

Directions: Look at the numbers inside the boxes. They go together in a certain way. Which answer choice would go inside the empty space in the bottom row?

Tips: See if you can spot the pattern that the design in each box has made, as you go from left to right.

There is also a pattern that goes up and down.

The last row must continue this pattern.

In the example, going across the first row, 6 is added to the number in the first column to get the number in the second column: 25 + 6 = 31. Then, 13 is added to get the number in the third column: 31 + 13 = 44.

Down the columns, 7 is added to the top number to get the bottom number: 25 + 7 = 32 and 44 + 7 = 51.

EXAMPLE

25	31	44
32	?	51

A 34   B 51   C 38   D 48   E 39

45

42	6	24
7	1	4
?	5	20

A 60   B 35   C 70   D 28   E 30

46

32	8	13
36	9	14
40	?	15

A 10   B 15   C 20   D 38   E 30

47

60	12	2
30	6	?
90	18	3

A 10   B 5   C 2   D 1   E 3

48

17	9	1
20	12	4
16	?	0

A 10   B 52   C 22   D 18   E 8

NUMERIC INFERENCES

Directions: Look at the first two sets of numbers. The numbers in each set belong together in a certain way. Look at the last set. A number is missing. Which answer choice would go with the number(s) in the last set in the same way that the first two sets go together?

Tips: Use the same methodology to complete Numeric Inferences as you used for Figure Analogies and Verbal Analogies.

Work through these together so your test-taker sees how the first two sets are related.

Together, come up with a "rule" to describe how they are related. Take this "rule," use it together with the missing number in the last set, and figure out which of the answer choices would follow that same rule.

In the example, in each set 13 is added to the first number to get the second number: 9 + 13 = 22, 12 + 13 = 25, and 42 + 13 = 55.

Then, to go from the second number to the third number you subtract 8: 22 - 8 = 14, 25 - 8 = 17, and 55 - 8 = ?. Can you figure out the answer?

EXAMPLE

1   [9, 22, 14]   [12, 25, 17]   [42, 55, ?]

   A 14   B 48   C 56   D 47   E 27

49 [4, 16]   [12, 48]   [7, ?]

A 32   B 80   C 75   D 40   E 28

50 [12, 36, 33]   [6, 18, 15]   [10, 30, ?]

A 23   B 27   C 33   D 90   E 55

51 [219, 250, 750]   [69, 100, 300]   [149, 180, ?]

A 140   B 480   C 540   D 470   E 270

52 [6, 24, 32]   [8, 32, 40]   [11, 44, ?]

A 45   B 52   C 11   D 30   E 50

NUMERIC SERIES

Directions: Which answer choice would complete the pattern?

Tips: Here, you must figure out a pattern that the numbers have made.

It could involve adding, subtracting, multiplying, or dividing. It could change from one number to the next.

In between each set of numbers, try figure out what has changed and write it in between the two numbers.

Look at the example below.

How would you go from 33333 to 44444? In this series, it is important to see that the numbers come in pairs.

In each pair, the first number has all 3s and the next number has all 4s.

Each pair loses one digit compared to the previous pair.

Therefore, the next number should be 33.

| 33333 | 44444 | 3333 | 4444 | 333 | 444 | ? |

Ⓐ 33   Ⓑ 3   Ⓒ 444   Ⓓ 2   Ⓔ 43

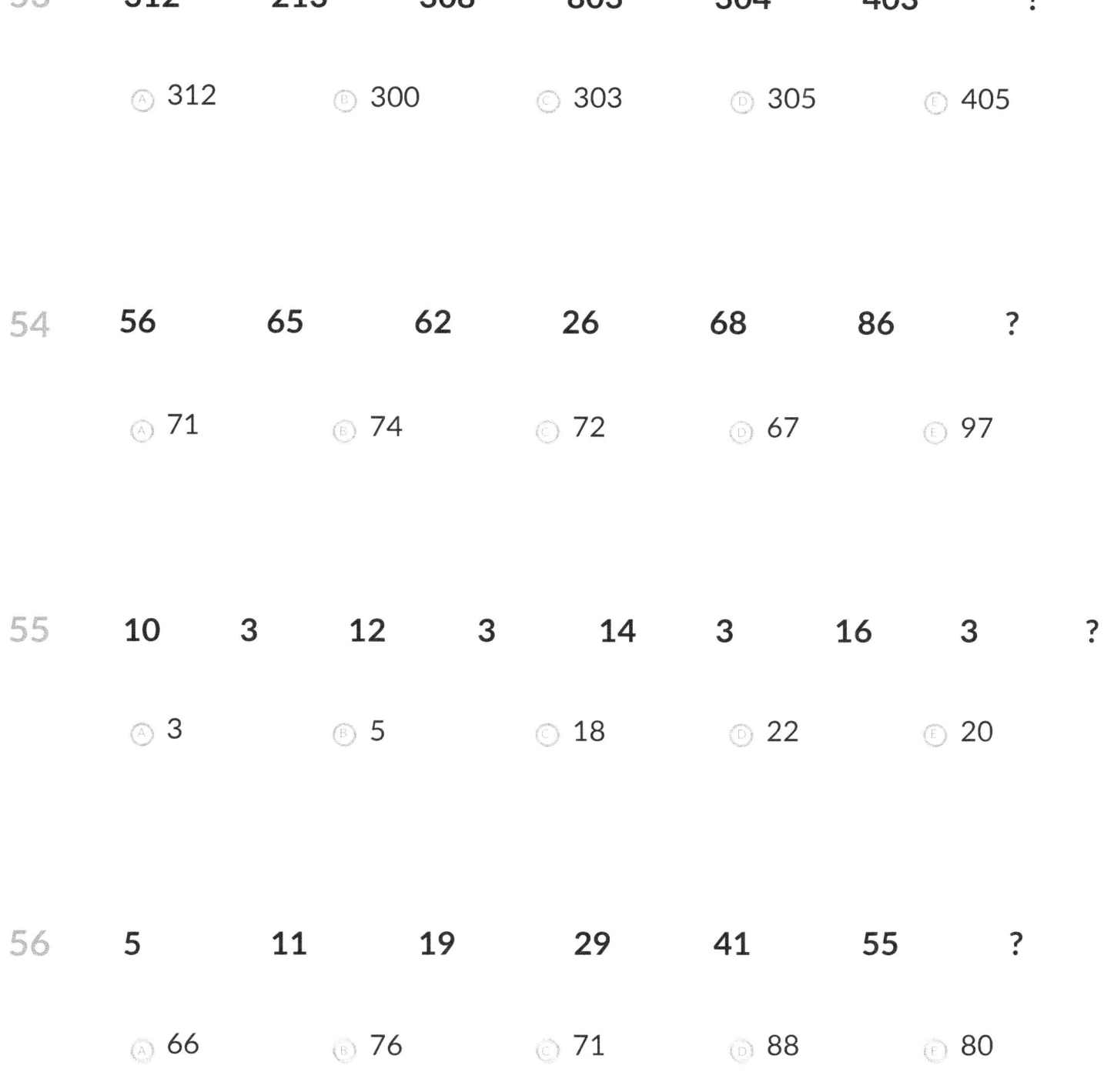

53   **312**   **213**   **308**   **803**   **304**   **403**   **?**

Ⓐ 312   Ⓑ 300   Ⓒ 303   Ⓓ 305   Ⓔ 405

54   **56**   **65**   **62**   **26**   **68**   **86**   **?**

Ⓐ 71   Ⓑ 74   Ⓒ 72   Ⓓ 67   Ⓔ 97

55   **10**   **3**   **12**   **3**   **14**   **3**   **16**   **3**   **?**

Ⓐ 3   Ⓑ 5   Ⓒ 18   Ⓓ 22   Ⓔ 20

56   **5**   **11**   **19**   **29**   **41**   **55**   **?**

Ⓐ 66   Ⓑ 76   Ⓒ 71   Ⓓ 88   Ⓔ 80

- Practice Test 2 Begins On The Next Page -

*Note: Questions in Practice Test 2 & 3 are <u>not</u> grouped by question type (unlike Practice Test 1). When your student takes the actual test, questions will most likely not be grouped by question type.

PRACTICE TEST 2

1 The opposite of "include" is _____.

A accept   B exclude   C involve   D seclude   E incorporate

---

2 The words below must be arranged to make the best sentence. Which letter would the <u>last</u> word of the sentence begin with? Here are the words:

work   store   brand   she   will   the   at   new

A W   B S   C I   D O   E T

---

3 What number is ten less than one-third of ninety?

A 20   B 28   C 30   D 33   E 35

---

4 Which choice makes the second set of pictures go together in the same way as the first set?

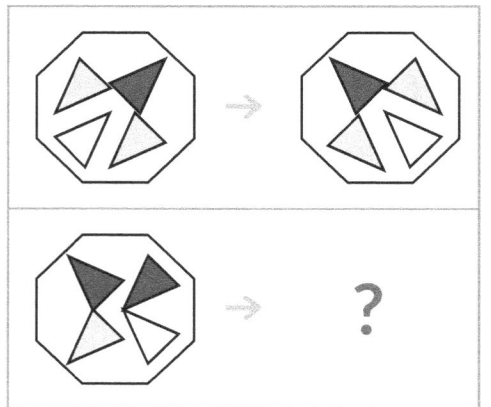

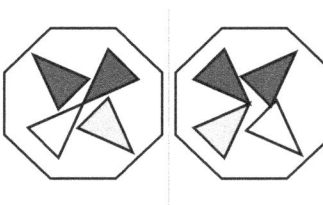 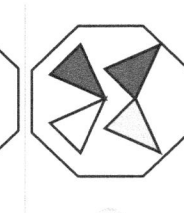 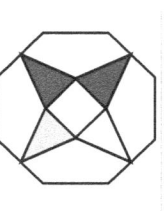 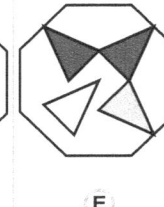

A   B   C   D   E

5   "Stagnant" is the opposite of _____.

   A flowing   B inactive   C motionless   D sluggish   E stationary

6   A team must always have _____.

   A uniforms   B a coach   C members   D a team name   E equipment

7   Which word does not go with the others?

   A trench   B trough   C abyss   D peak   E valley

8   Which word does not go with the others?

   A silo   B vault   C cellar   D mantle   E warehouse

9   Which answer choice makes the second set of words go together in the
     same way that the first set does?

   metal > fragment : bread > ?

   A loaf   B slice   C crust   D dough   E crumb

10 The words below need to be arranged to make the best sentence. Which letter would the <u>last</u> word of the sentence begin with? Here are the words:

a by campers the were almost venomous bitten snake

- A A
- B B
- C S
- D W
- E V

---

11 Samantha bought 3 packs of green markers, 2 packs of yellow markers, and 4 packs of purple markers. If each pack contains 5 markers, how many markers did Samantha buy in total?

- A 55
- B 45
- C 54
- D 40
- E 50

---

12 Which choice makes the second set of pictures go together in the same way as the first set?

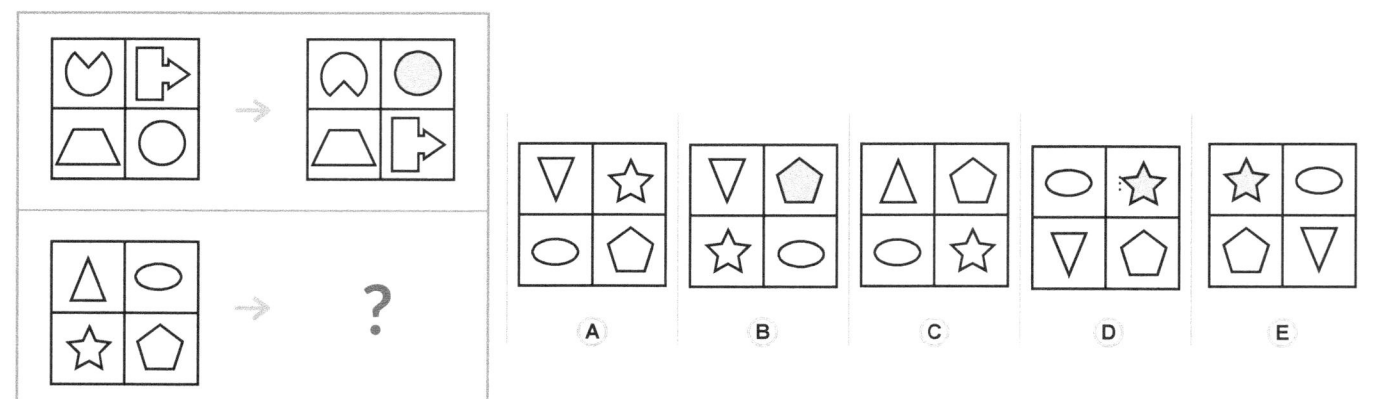

---

13 The numbers in the below box go together in a certain way. Which answer choice would replace the question mark?

| 42 | 35 | 44 |
| ? | 23 | 32 |

- A 35
- B 30
- C 32
- D 45
- E 28

14 Which answer choice best completes the sentence?

The students were _____ when they received the award for their hard work on the science project.

A curious   B neutral   C confused   D elated   E studious

15

rock	riddle	rope
mock	middle	?

A mope   B hope   C fiddle   D ropes   E most

16 Which answer choice makes the second set of words go together in the same way that the first set does?

artist > occupation : cathedral > ?

A altar   B plaza   C mansion   D monument   E sculpture

17 Which answer choice best completes the sentence?

Orchards and cornfields were _____ affected by the severe drought that struck the region last summer.

A slightly   B barely   C significantly   D somewhat   E minimally

18 What number should replace the question mark (?) so that all three sets of numbers go together in the same way?

[210, 420, 35]   [258, 516, 43]   [144, 288, ?]

A 44   B 24   C 28   D 32   E 12

19   The words below must be arranged to make the best sentence. Which letter would the __first__ word of the sentence begin with? Here are the words:

storm   several   from   caused   damage   debris   to   homes   the

- A S
- B H
- C C
- D D
- E F

20   What number is five more than seven times seven?

- A 48
- B 50
- C 52
- D 54
- E 56

21   A concert must always have _____.

- A performers
- B tickets
- C a stage
- D an audience
- E lights

22   Which answer choice makes the second set of words go together in the same way that the first set does?

alphabetical → letter : chronological → ?

- A pattern
- B list
- C time
- D calendar
- E chronicle

23   Which answer choice makes the second set of words go together in the same way that the first set does?

boulder → pebble : blaze → ?

- A smolder
- B vapor
- C parched
- D extinguish
- E flame

24 The words below need to be arranged to make the best sentence. Which letter would the <u>first</u> word of the sentence begin with? Here are the words:

keep   ships   water   in   have   chains   that   anchors   the   stable

A A   B T   C C   D W   E K

---

25 All parks must have _____.

A benches   B trees   C walking paths   D open space   E fountains

---

26 Which answer choice makes the second set of words go together in the same way that the first set does?

dense → mass : bright → ?

A dark   B opaque   C light   D dazzling   E intensity

---

27 Which answer choice makes the second set of words go together in the same way that the first set does?

mountain → summit : pyramid → ?

A base   B apex   C lateral   D edge   E triangle

---

28 The words in the below box go together in a certain way. Which answer choice would go in place of the question mark?

cot	cat	coat
bat	bit	?

A bite   B bode   C code   D bait   E but

29 "Acquire" is the opposite of ____.

(A) assemble   (B) obtain   (C) operate   (D) lose   (E) require

---

30 Which answer choice best completes the sentence?

Because the soil was extremely _____, the crops failed to grow properly in the area.

(A) hydrated   (B) productive   (C) fertile   (D) organic   (E) depleted

---

31 Sarah had 20 marbles. She gave 5 marbles to her friend. Then, she lost 4 marbles, but she found 3 marbles on the ground. How many marbles does Sarah have now?

(A) 10   (B) 11   (C) 12   (D) 13   (E) 14

---

32 A camera always has a ____.

(A) lens   (B) tripod   (C) film   (D) flash

---

33 The numbers below form a pattern. What number should go in place of the question mark to continue the pattern?

3   4   7   12   19   28   ?

(A) 36   (B) 37   (C) 38   (D) 27   (E) 39

34 "Ambiguously" is the opposite of ____.

A uncertainty   B vaguely   c obscurely   D clearly   E anonymously

35 Which answer choice best completes the sentence?

"When you explore this area of the forest, avoid the spots with _____ terrain," the park ranger _____ the hikers.

A formidable, instructed   B uniform, suggested   c captivating, recommended   D ordinary, guided   E alluring, recommended

36 Which word does not go with the others?

A hibernate   B hover   c depart   D stagnate   E dwell

37 Which word does not go with the others?

A ascend   B migrate   c evacuate   D circumnavigate   E ponder

38 Which answer choice makes the second set of words go together in the same way that the first set does?

adorn > decorate : refute > ?

A argue   B confirm   c concede   D disprove   E defend

39 The numbers below form a pattern. What number should go in place of the question mark to continue the pattern?

222   210   200   192   186   182   ?

A 130   B 180   C 142   D 174   E 182

40 The words in the below box go together in a certain way. Which answer choice would go in place of the question mark?

fe	ft	feet
go	gd	?

A geese   B golf   C god   D feed   E good

---

41 Which choice makes the second set of pictures go together in the same way as the first set?

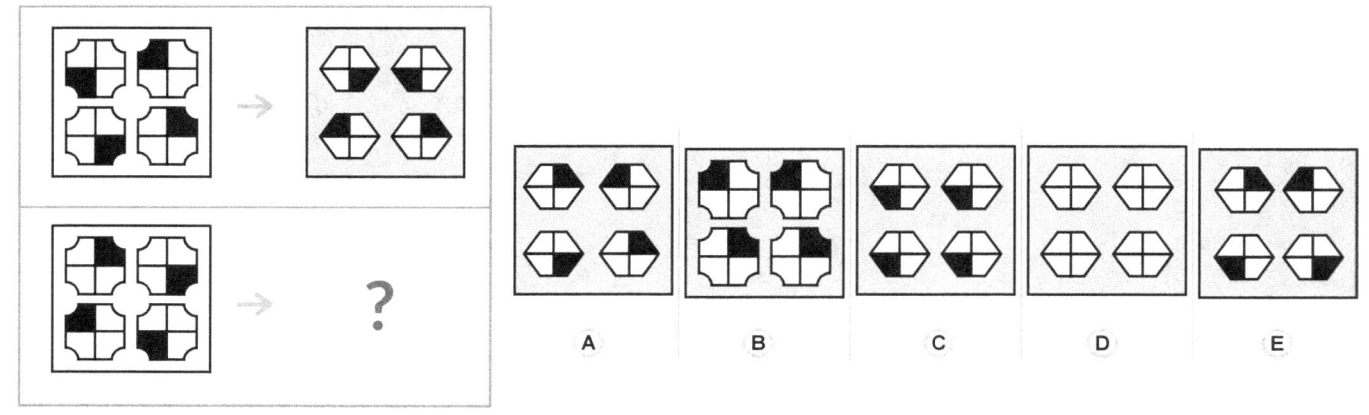

---

42 Which answer choice makes the second set of words go together in the same way that the first set does?

atom > molecule : verse > ?

A word   B illustration   C table of contents   D poem   E rhyme

---

43 What number comes next in the series?

2   3   5   8   13   21   34   ?

A 43   B 53   C 50   D 57   E 55

44 The words in the below box go together in a certain way. Which answer choice would go in place of the question mark?

ancient	victory	frail
modern	defeat	?

A fragile   B strong   C delicate   D clever   E rapid

45 Which choice makes the second set of pictures go together in the same way as the first set?

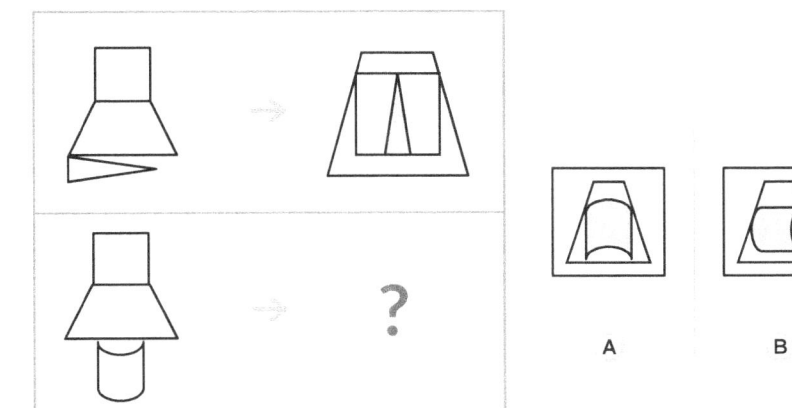

 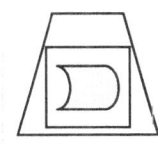 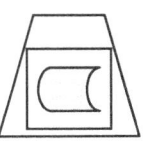 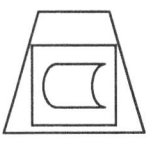

A   B   C   D   E

46 What number should replace the question mark (?) so that all three sets of numbers go together in the same way?

[226, 571]   [332, 677]   [318, ?]

A 663   B 676   C 765   D 735   E 616

47 What number comes next in the series?

2   -2   4   -4   6   -6   ?

A 7   B -7   C 8   D -8   E 9

48 The numbers in the below box go together in a certain way. Which answer choice would replace the question mark?

41	63	85
?	50	72

A 43   B 34   C 28   D 53   E 27

49 What comes next in the series?

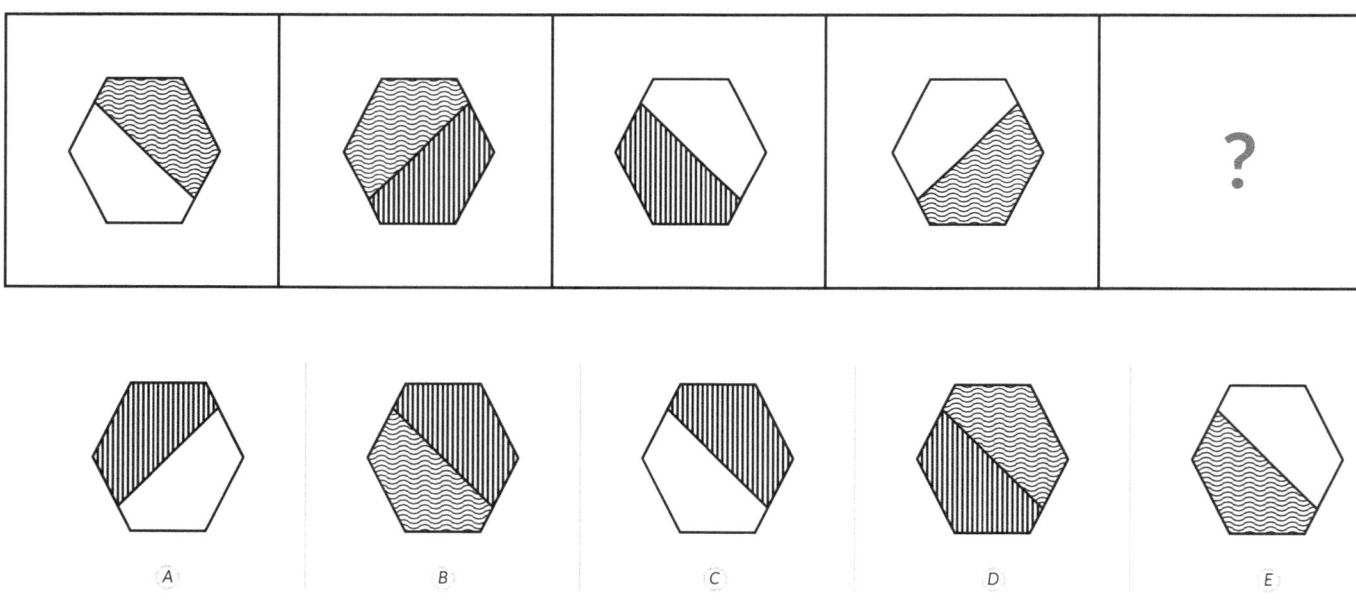

50

The numbers in the below box go together in a certain way. Which answer choice would replace the question mark?

232	274	221
?	235	182
148	190	137

A 165   B 234   C 195   D 178   E 193

51

What comes next in the series?

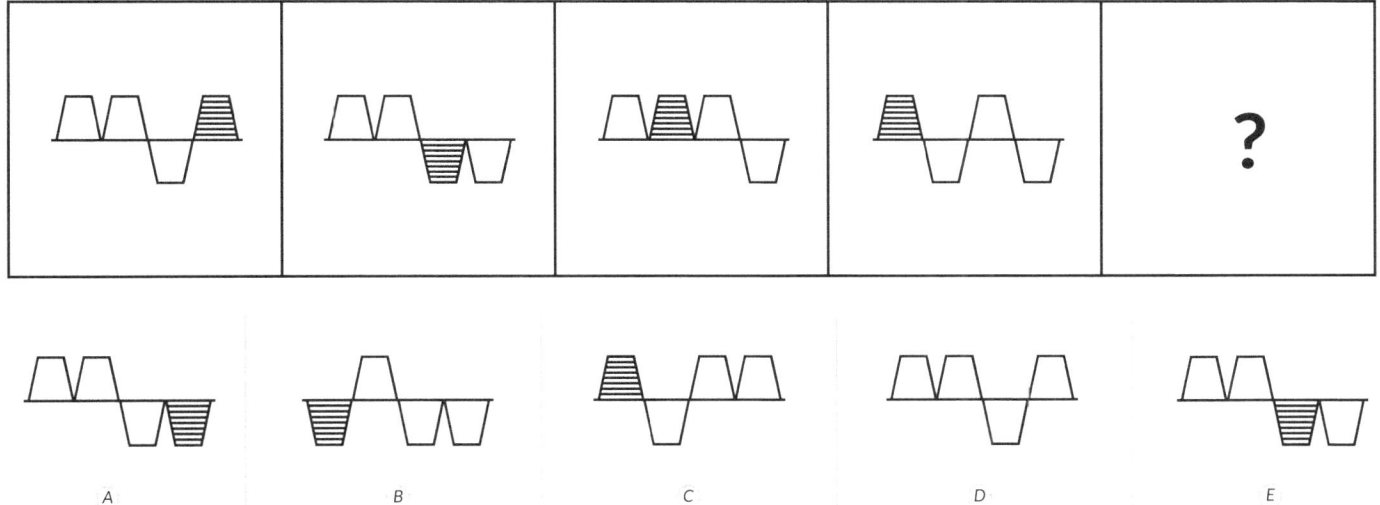

A   B   C   D   E

52

The numbers in the below box go together in a certain way. Which answer choice would replace the question mark?

62	35	96
96	?	130
67	40	101

A 66   B 67   C 69   D 60   E 72

53 **What comes next in the series?**

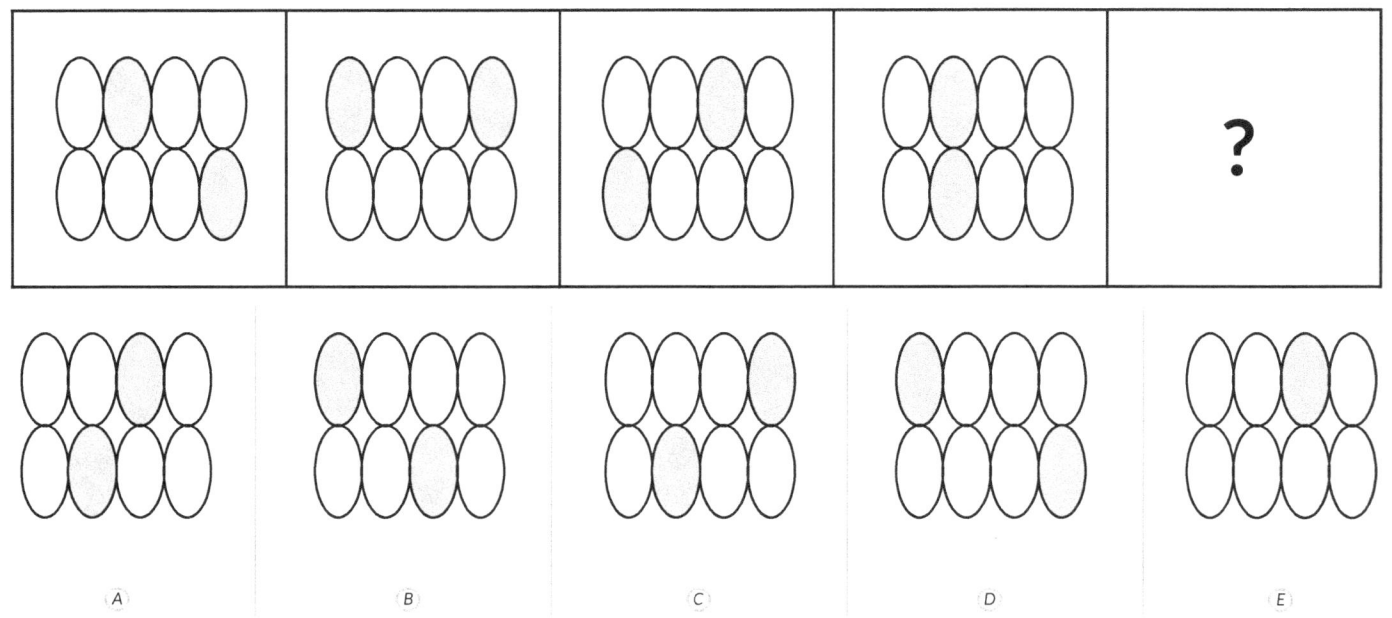

54 **The objects in the boxes go together in a certain way. What goes in the empty box?**

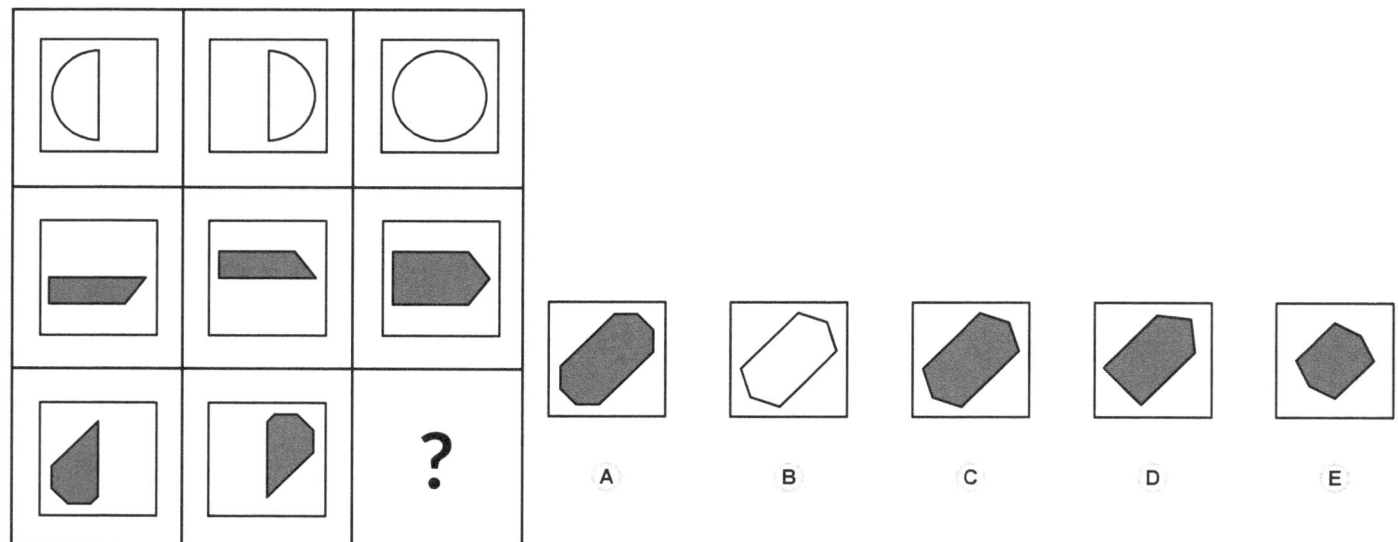

55   **What comes next in the series?**

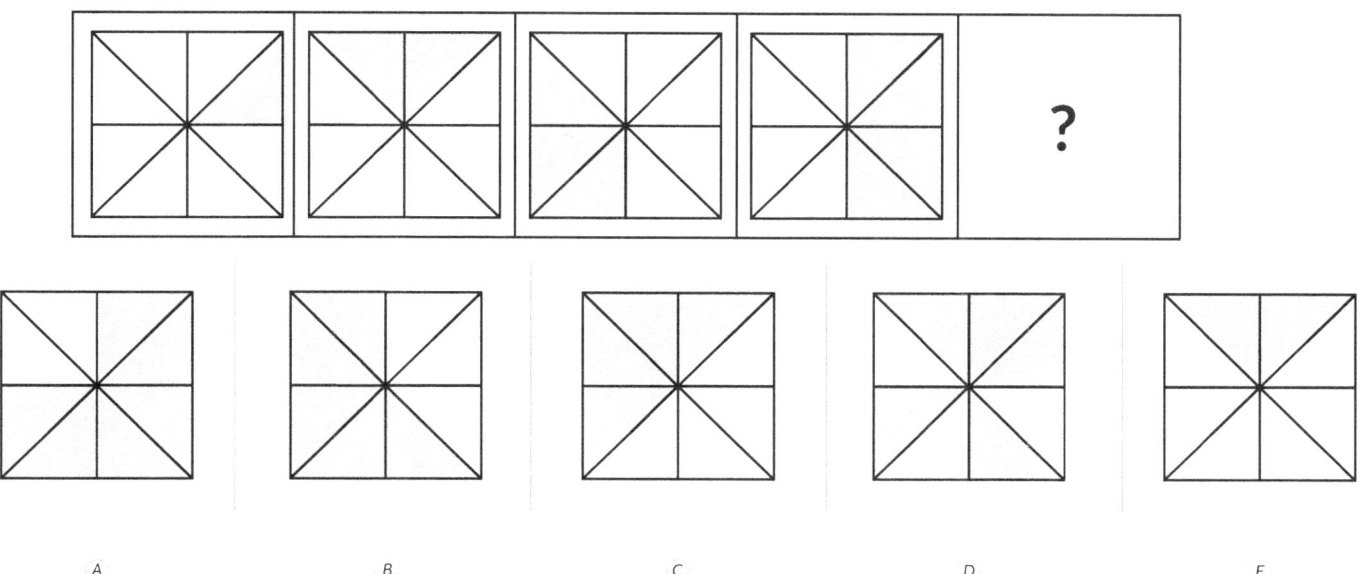

A   B   C   D   E

56   **The objects in the boxes go together in a certain way. What goes in the empty box?**

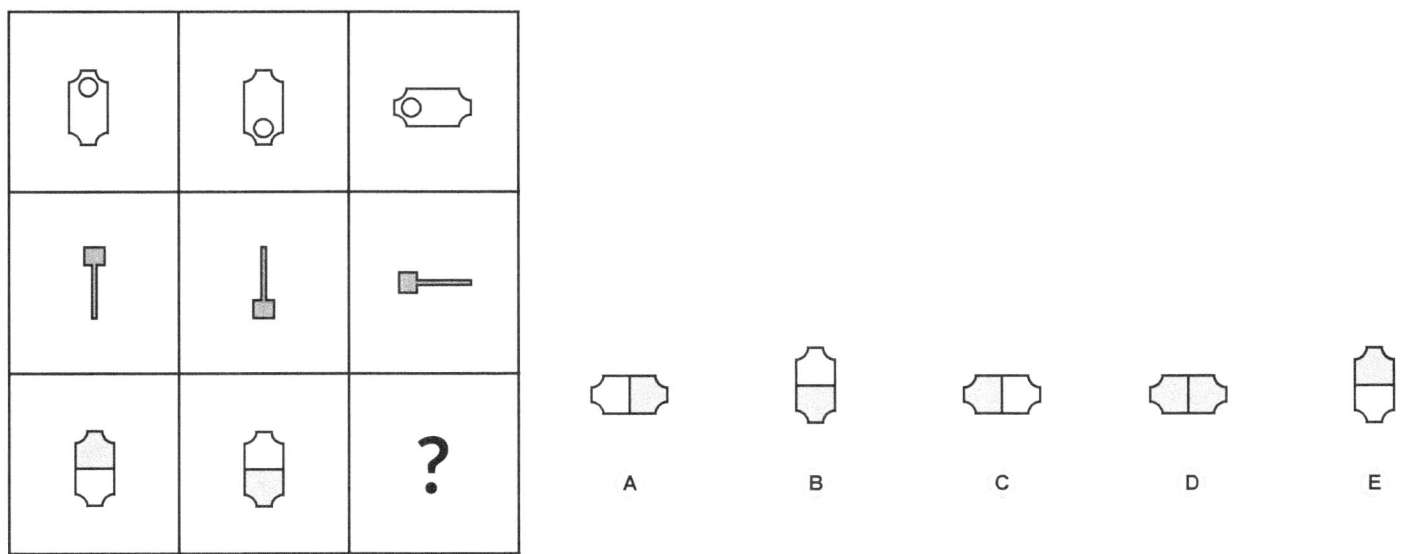

A   B   C   D   E

57 The objects in the boxes go together in a certain way. What goes in the empty box?

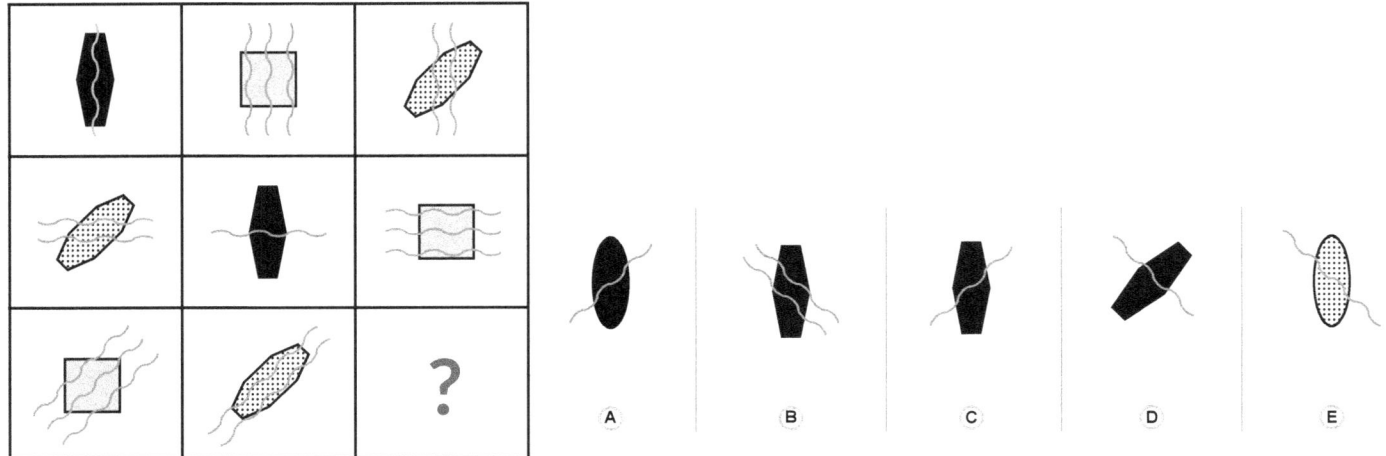

A   B   C   D   E

58 What comes next in the series?

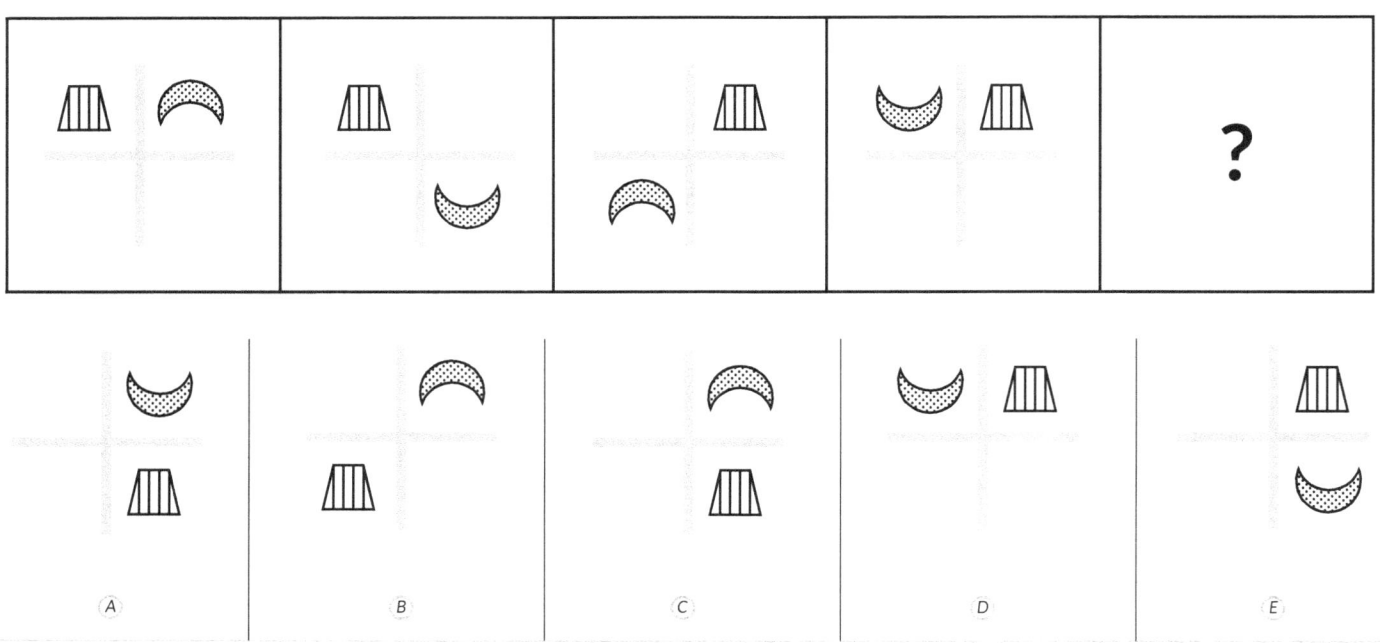

A   B   C   D   E

59 What number should replace the question mark (?) so that all three sets of numbers go together in the same way?

[24, 39, 23]   [41, 56, 40]   [72, ?, 71]

A 88   B 78   C 74   D 87   E 92

60 **The objects in the boxes go together in a certain way. What goes in the empty box?**

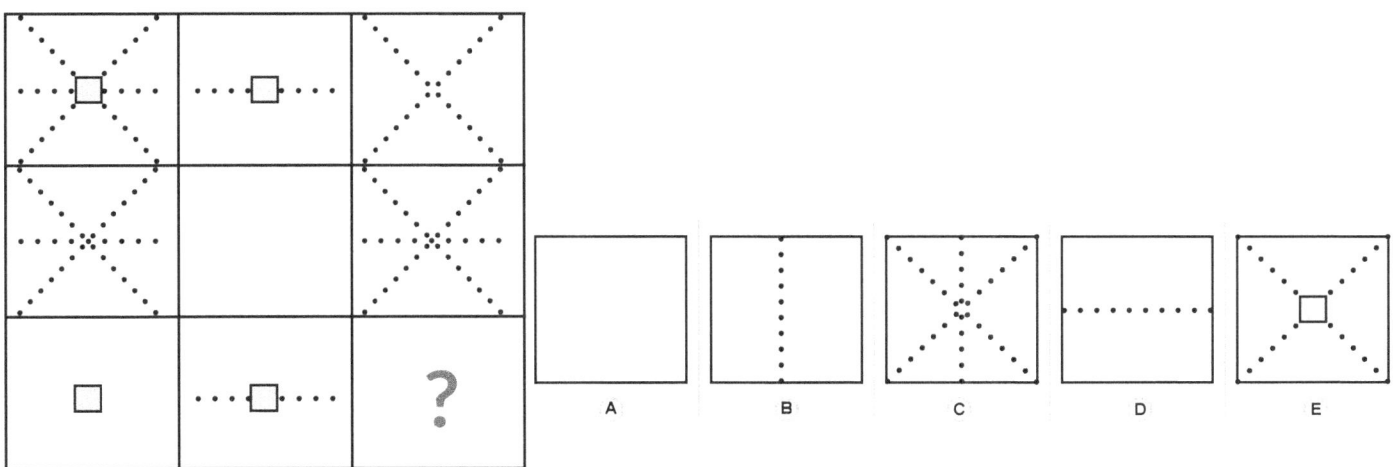

61 **The objects in the boxes go together in a certain way. What goes in the empty box?**

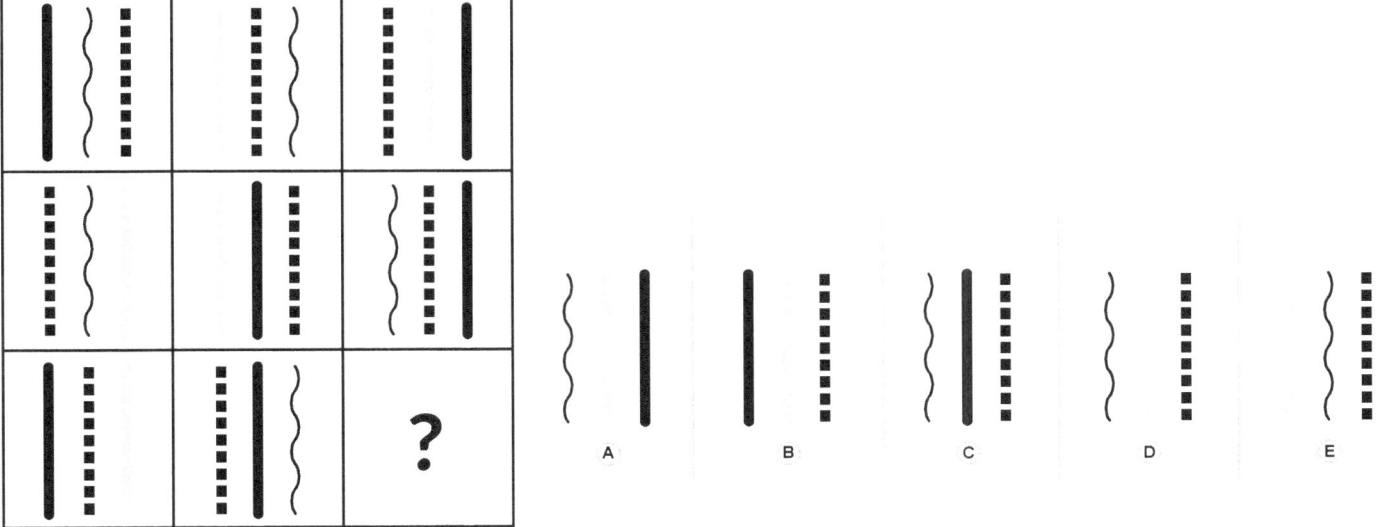

62 **What number should replace the question mark (?) so that all three sets of numbers go together in the same way?**

[11, 77, 44]   [13, 91, 58]   [9, ?, 30]

A 56   B 65   c 63   D 78   E 72

63 Elisa has more books than Daniel. Sophia has more books than Rachel. Olivia has fewer books than Daniel but more books than Rachel. Which of the following <u>must</u> be true?

    (A) Sophia has more books than Olivia.

    (B) Rachel has more books than Olivia.

    (C) Elisa has more books than Sophia.

    (D) Daniel has more books than Rachel.

    (E) Olivia has more books than Daniel.

64 Sarah has a higher grade than Tom. Lily has a higher grade than James, but not as high as Maria. Sarah has a higher grade than James, but not as high as Lily. Which of the following is true?

    (A) Maria has the highest grade.

    (B) Tom has a higher grade than James.

    (C) Sarah has the highest grade.

    (D) James has the lowest grade.

    (E) Tom has the highest grade.

65 Which choice makes the second set of pictures go together in the same way as the first set?

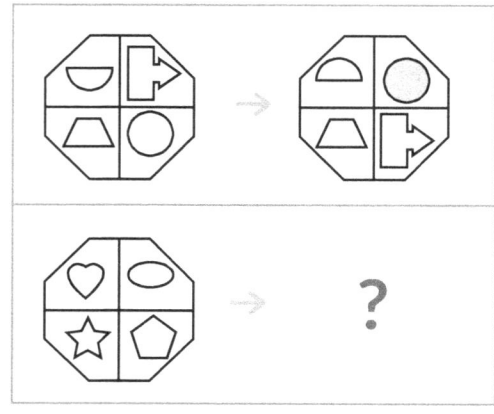

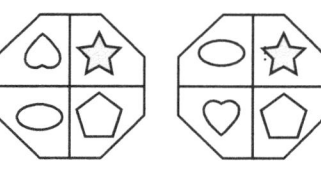   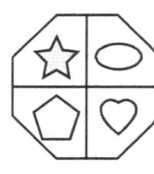

A   B   C   D   E

66 What number comes next in the series?

32   33   34   36   37   38   40   41   ?

42   44   43   45   46

67 What number comes next in the series?

5   10   11   22   23   ?

44   45   46   47   48

68 What number comes next in the series?

5   20   10   40   20   ?

10   100   40   120   80

69 Which answer choice makes the second set of words go together in the same way that the first set does?

ameliorate > improve : condense > ?

A dissolve   B expand   C align   D magnify   E compress

70 Which answer choice makes the second set of words go together in the same way that the first set does?

negligence > accident : disease > ?

A health   B cure   C epidemic   D hospital   E crash

PRACTICE TEST 3

1   **"Exhaust" is the opposite of _____.**

    Ⓐ deplete   Ⓑ fatigue   Ⓒ replenish   Ⓓ moderate   Ⓔ maintain

2   **Olivia's aunt gave her fifty dollars to spend on a new outfit. Olivia bought a shirt for twenty-five dollars, spent eight dollars on flip-flops, and bought a hat for ten dollars. How much money did Olivia have left?**

    Ⓐ $2   Ⓑ $3   Ⓒ $5   Ⓓ $7   Ⓔ $10

3   **What number comes next in the series?**

    12.5   9.5   5.5   0.5   -5.5   -12.5   -20.5   ?

    Ⓐ 29.5   Ⓑ 30.5   Ⓒ -29.5   Ⓓ -31.5   Ⓔ -30.5

4   **What number should replace the question mark (?) so that all three sets of numbers go together in the same way?**

    [11, 66, 396]   [3, 18, 108]   [4, ?, 144]

    Ⓐ 72   Ⓑ 36   Ⓒ 24   Ⓓ 30   Ⓔ 66

5 "Productive" is the opposite of _____.

A idle B efficient C fruitful D instructive E constructive

6 What number is four more than the square root of sixteen?

A 4 B 8 C 10 D 12 E 14

7 What number comes next in the series?

4 4 4 4 8 16 8 24 72 ?

A 18 B 24 C 36 D 48 E 54

8 What number should replace the question mark (?) so that all three sets of numbers go together in the same way?

[121, 214] [165, 258] [108, ?]

A 201 B 126 C 210 D 243 E 165

9 The opposite of "compassionate" is _____.

    (A) encompassing   (B) empathetic   (C) generous   (D) ignorant   (E) unkind

---

10 Which choice makes the second set of pictures go together in the same way as the first set?

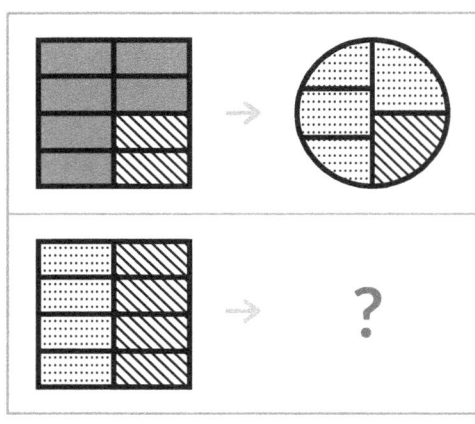
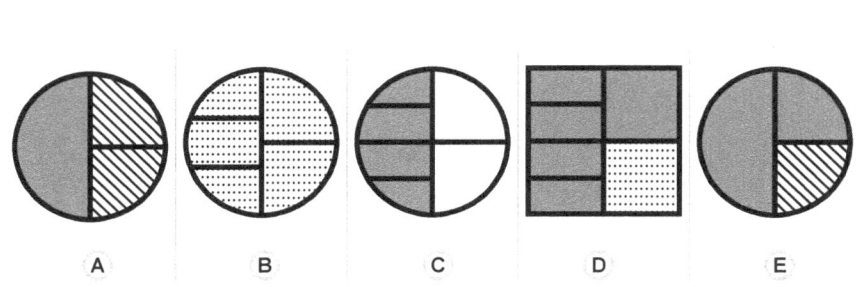

    A   B   C   D   E

---

11 What number should replace the question mark (?) so that all three sets of numbers go together in the same way?

[379, 295]   [756, 672]   [457, ?]

  (A) 345   (B) 426   (C) 373   (D) 576   (E) 432

---

12 The numbers in the below box go together in a certain way. Which answer choice would replace the question mark?

396	217	179
658	394	264
262	?	85

  (A) 166   (B) 167   (C) 188   (D) 177   (E) 187

13 "Converge" is the opposite of _____.

   A quantify   B intersect   C separate   D evaluate   E verge

14 Which choice makes the second set of pictures go together in the same way as the first set?

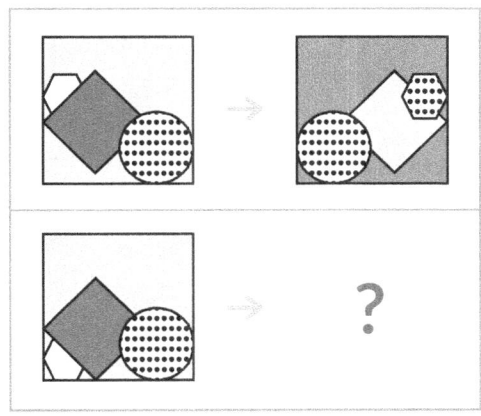 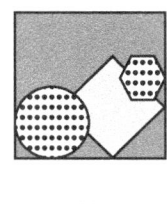 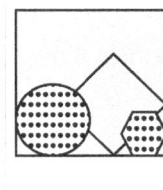 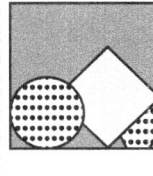 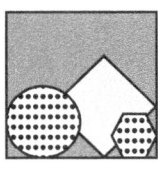 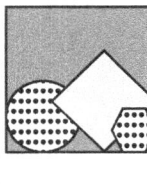

      A   B   C   D   E

15 What number should replace the question mark (?) so that all three sets of numbers go together in the same way?

[516, 333, 849]   [478, 124, 602]   [493, 142, ?]

   A 765   B 498   C 740   D 635   E 665

16 What number comes next in the series?

-3   -7   -9   2   -27   11 ?

   A -16   B -81   C -54   D 20   E 81

17 The words below need to be arranged to make the best sentence. Which letter would the <u>last</u> word of the sentence begin with? Here are the words:

keep   have   soil   roots   that   them   anchored   trees   in   the

(A) S   (B) T   (C) R   (D) H   (E) K

---

18 All hotels must have _____.

(A) a swimming pool   (B) rooms   (C) a restaurant   (D) a concierge   (E) wi-fi

---

19 The words in the below box go together in a certain way. Which answer choice would replace the question mark?

storm	rain	strain
sling	ant	?

(A) slant   (B) shade   (C) shape   (D) sharp   (E) stain

---

20 What number should replace the question mark (?) so that all three sets of numbers go together in the same way?

[1, 8]   [11, 88]   [88, ?]

(A) 808   (B) 1118   (C) 888   (D) 704   (E) 99

21 The words below need to be arranged to make the best sentence. Which letter would the <u>first</u> word of the sentence begin with? Here are the words:

place   keep   frames   have   that   glasses   the   lenses   in

A P   B T   C F   D L   E G

22 Which answer choice best completes the sentence?

To ensure accurate results, it is important to use _____ methods for analyzing the data.

A random   B experimental   C precise   D inconsistent   E optional

23 All banks have _____.

A tellers   B vaults   C money   D ATMs   E checks

24 What number should replace the question mark (?) so that all three sets of numbers go together in the same way?

[665, 384, 128]   [593, 312, 104]   [545, 264, ?]

A 78   B 98   C 47   D 76   E 88

25 The words below need to be arranged to make the best sentence. Which letter would the <u>first</u> word of the sentence begin with? Here are the words:

attack ferocious by the avoided an hikers a bear exhausted

- A A
- B B
- C F
- D T
- E E

26 Which answer choice best completes the sentence?

The state's array of _____ parks appeals to those searching for unspoiled wilderness.

- A urban
- B cultivated
- C theme
- D congested
- E pristine

27 What number should replace the question mark (?) so that all three sets of numbers go together in the same way?

[1, 1]   [2, 8]   [4, ?]

- A 16
- B 27
- C 64
- D 81
- E 100

28 All airports have a _____.

- A baggage claim
- B security checkpoint
- C control tower
- D runway
- E restaurant

29 What number comes next in the series?

-2.5   -3.5   -1.5   -4.5   -8.5   -3.5   -9.5   -16.5   -8.5 ?

- A -9.5
- B -18.5
- C -19.5
- D -16.5
- E -17.5

30 The words below need to be arranged to make the best sentence. Which letter would the <u>first</u> word of the sentence begin with? Here are the words:

storm   grow   rain   from   to   a   plants   enabled

A P   B S   C F   D R   E G

31 Which answer choice best completes the sentence?

One challenge with hiking is that it becomes more _____ as you ascend to higher _____ .

A demanding, depths   B unpredictable, troughs   C attainable, levels   D strenuous, altitudes   E relaxing, ridges

32 What number should replace the question mark (?) so that all three sets of numbers go together in the same way?

[24, 3]   [32, 5]   [8, ?]

A -2   B -1   C 2   D -13   E 5

33 A plant must always have _____.

A flowers   B leaves   C cells   D stems   E soil

34 What number comes next in the series?

4   4   4   4   8   16   8   24   72 ?

A 18   B 24   C 36   D 48   E 54

35 Which answer choice makes the second set of words go together in the same way that the first set does?

editor → revise : translator → ?

(A) restore   (B) interpret   (C) suppress   (D) simplify   (E) acknowledge

36 Which answer choice makes the second set of words go together in the same way that the first set does?

chisel → sculpture : scalpel → ?

(A) blade   (B) hospital   (C) surgeon   (D) surgery   (E) painting

37 Which word does not go with the others?

(A) tripod   (B) trilogy   (C) third   (D) trident   (E) thirst

38 Which word does not go with the others?

(A) author   (B) bibliography   (C) preface   (D) appendix   (E) index

39 The words in the below box go together in a certain way. Which answer choice would replace the question mark?

ve	lo	love
ap	tr	?

(A) lap   (B) velo   (C) part   (D) late   (E) trap

40 Which answer choice makes the second set of words go together in the same way that the first set does?

innovative → creativity : resolute → ?

A determination   B confusion   C uncertainty   D hesitation   E flexibility

41 Which answer choice makes the second set of words go together in the same way that the first set does?

infallible → error : immutable → ?

A mistake   B mute   C change   D delay   E stability

42 Which word does not go with the others?

A replicate   B imitate   C simulate   D develop   E mimic

43 Which word does not go with the others?

A sustain   B maintain   C prolong   D obstruct   E persist

44 The words in the below box go together in a certain way. Which answer choice would replace the question mark?

et	di	edit
tm	ea	?

A meat   B team   C mate   D eat   E emit

45 The words in the below box go together in a certain way. Which answer choice would replace the question mark?

desert	align	design
shade	mopes	?

   (A) sheen   (B) shapes   (C) shone   (D) ski   (E) song

46 Which choice makes the second set of pictures go together in the same way as the first set?

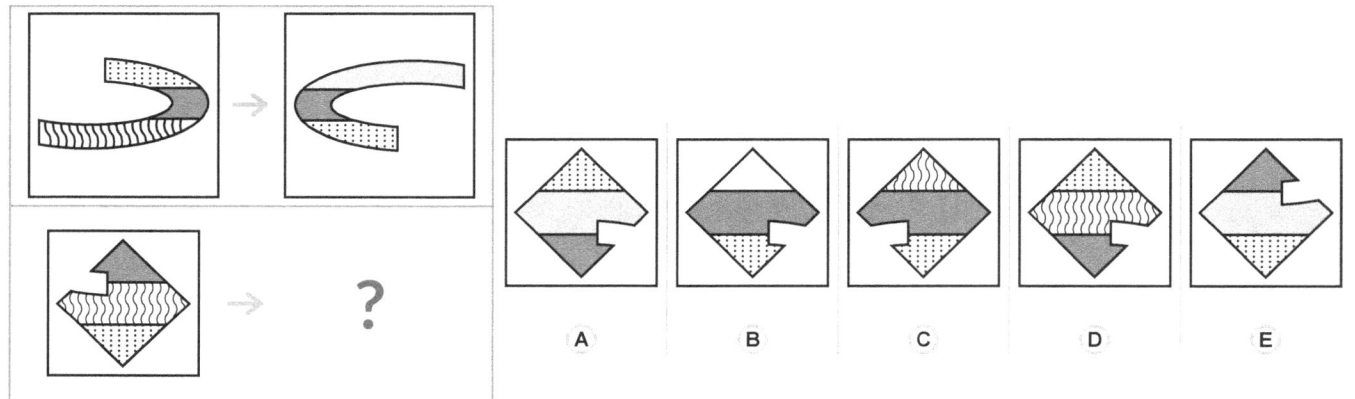

47 What number should replace the question mark (?) so that all three sets of numbers go together in the same way?

[16, 256]   [18, 324]   [19, ?]

   (A) 361   (B) 306   (C) 259   (D) 381   (E) 389

48 What number comes next in the series?

-3   0   -9   3   -27   6   ?

   (A) -30   (B) -81   (C) -54   (D) 81   (E) 34

49 The words in the below box go together in a certain way. Which answer choice would replace the question mark?

expand	complicate	abundant
contract	simplify	?

A generous   B rare   C explain   D adequate   E solid

50 Which choice makes the second set of pictures go together in the same way as the first set?

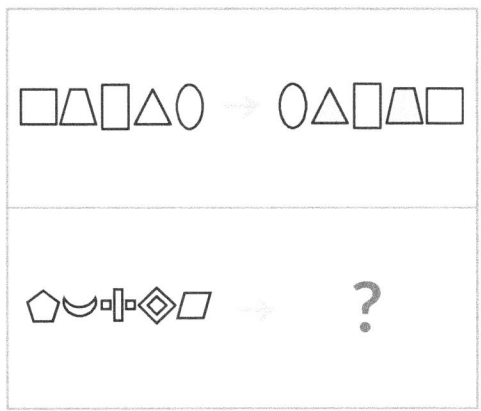

A

B

C

D

E

51 What number should replace the question mark (?) so that all three sets of numbers go together in the same way?

[2, 10]   [3, 29]   [4, ?]

A 66   B 64   C 62   D 30   E 12

52 The numbers in the below box go together in a certain way. Which answer choice would replace the question mark?

85	425	340
116	?	464
201	1,005	804

(A) 455   (B) 876   (C) 580   (D) 430   (E) 556

---

53 Which choice makes the second set of pictures go together in the same way as the first set?

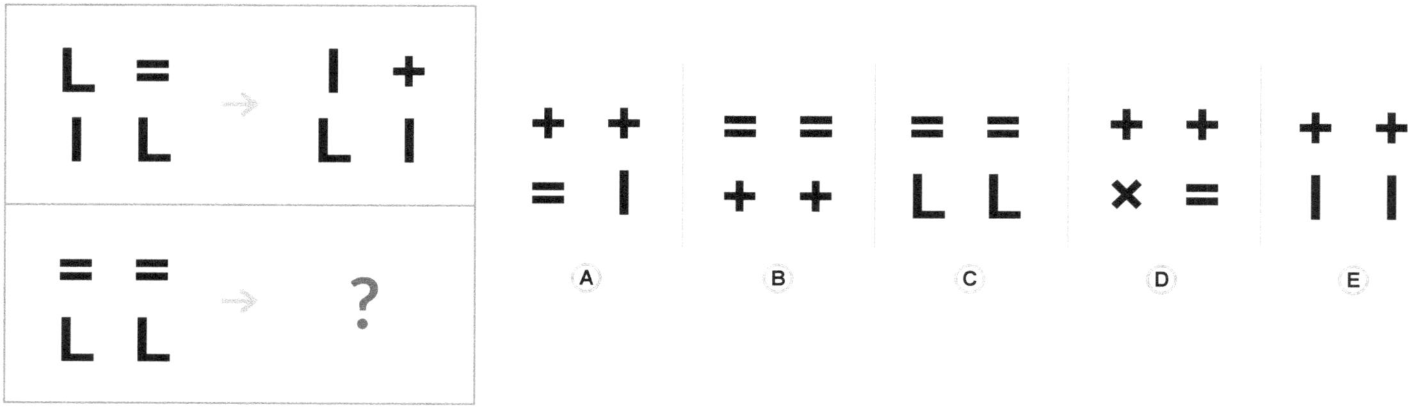

---

54 The numbers in the below box go together in a certain way. Which answer choice would replace the question mark?

366	342	708
61	?	118

(A) 55   (B) 50   (C) 69   (D) 57   (E) 60

55   Which answer choice would replace the question mark?

60	120	30
?	960	240
96	192	48

A 68   B 450   C 488   D 432   E 480

56   The objects in the boxes go together in a certain way.
What goes in the empty box?

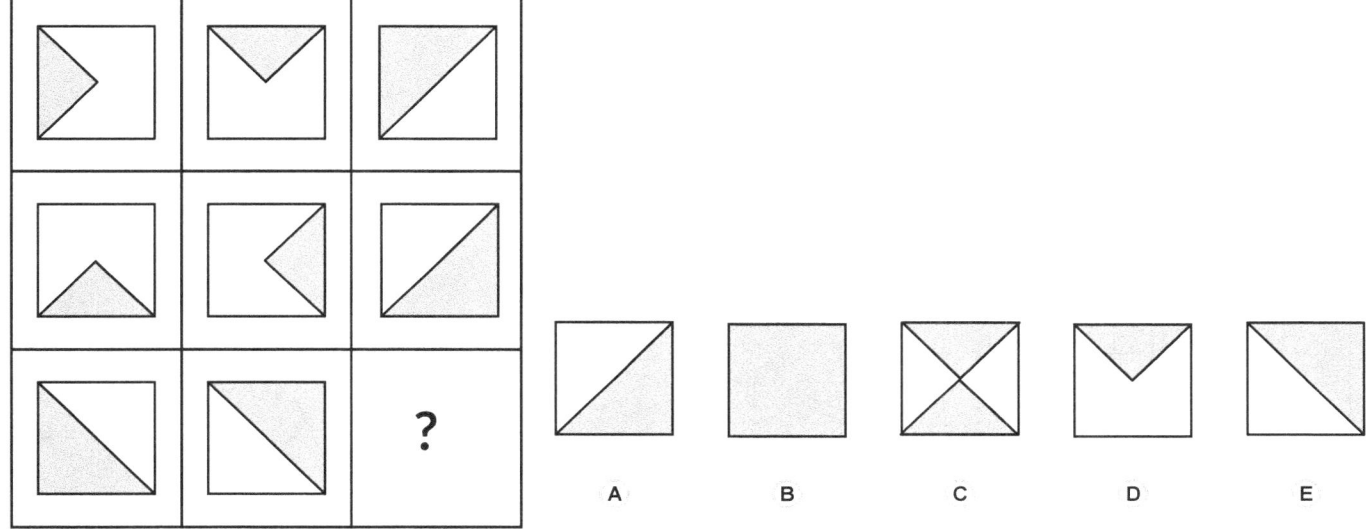

57   What comes next in the series?

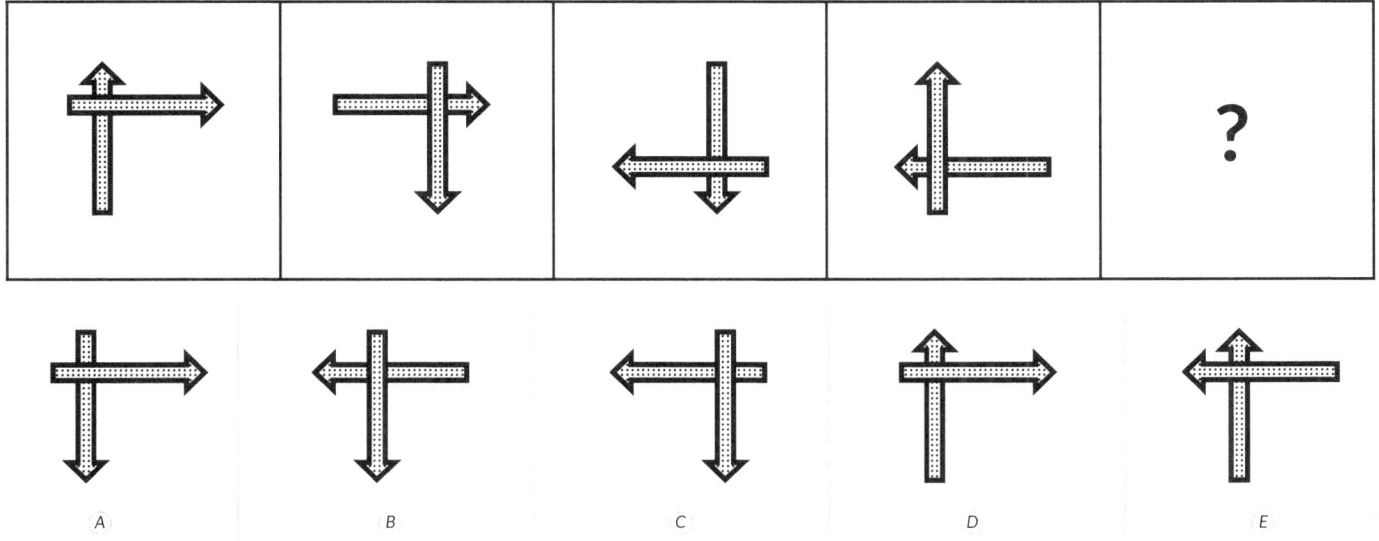

58 The objects in the boxes go together in a certain way.
What goes in the empty box?

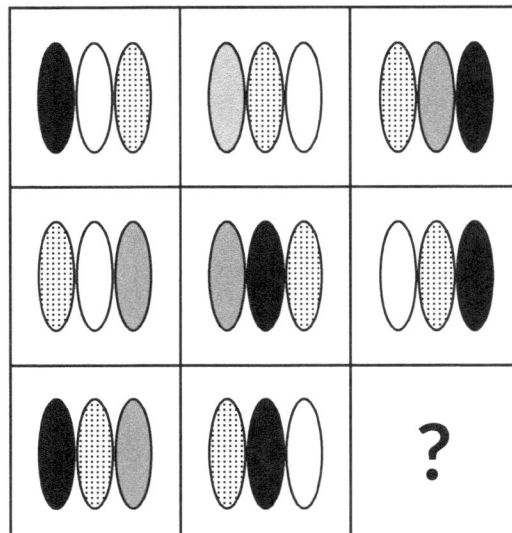

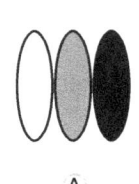   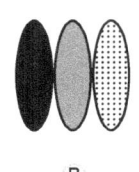   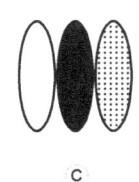   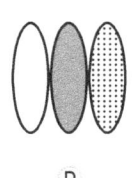   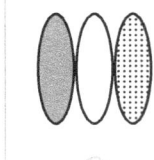

A   B   C   D   E

59 The objects in the boxes go together in a certain way.
What goes in the empty box?

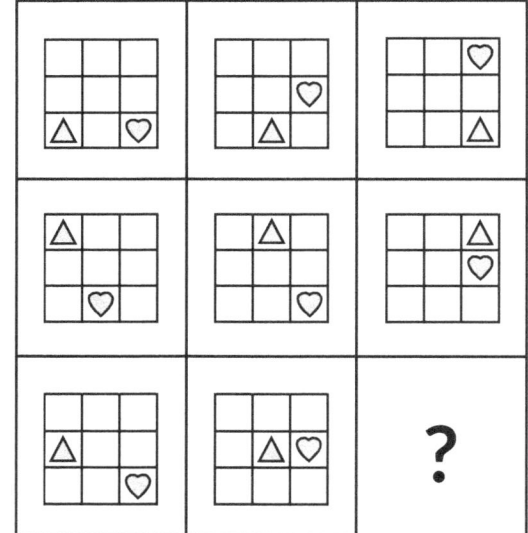

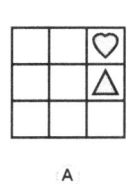   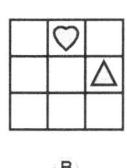   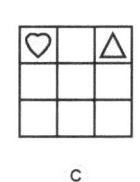   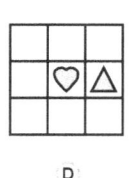

A   B   C   D   E

60 What number comes next in the series?

1   3   9   27   ?

○ 54   ○ 30   ○ 81   ○ 61   ○ 3

61 The objects in the boxes go together in a certain way.
What goes in the empty box?

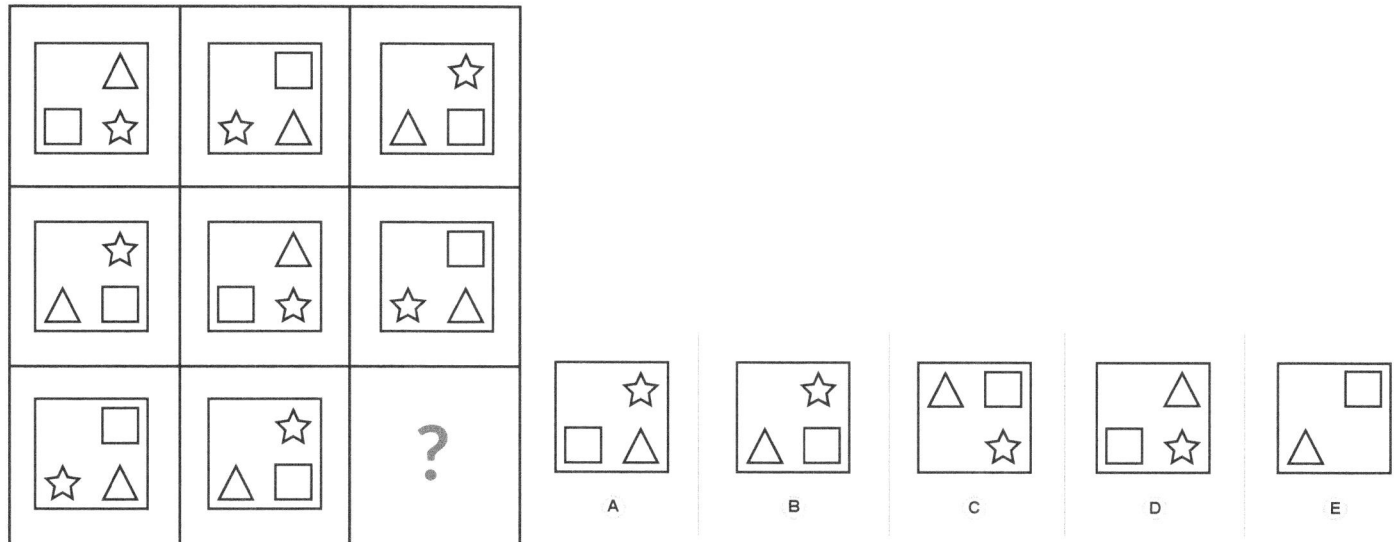

62 Which choice makes the second set of pictures go together in the same
way as the first set?

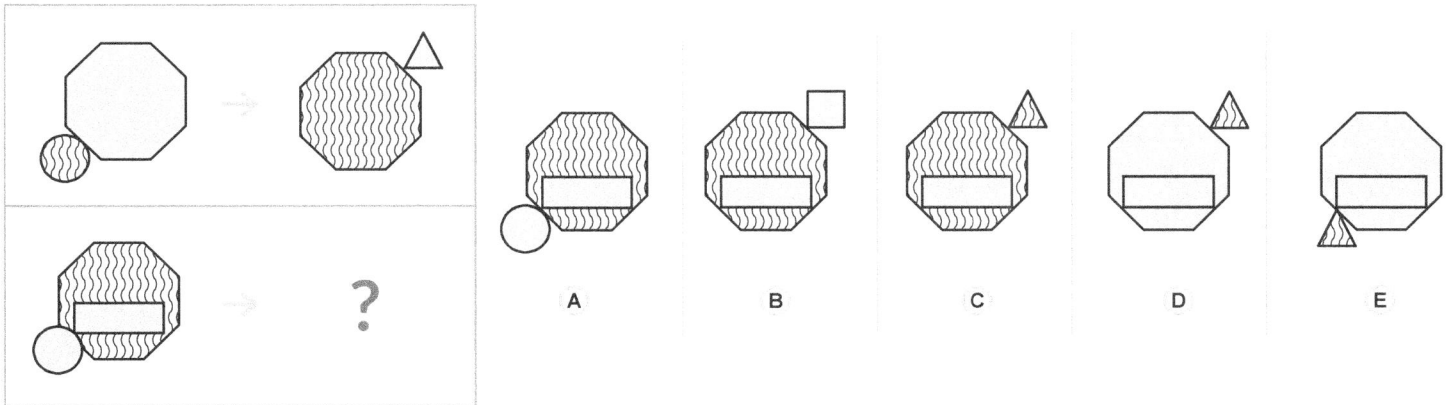

63 What number comes next in the series?

| 2 | 21 | 40 | 59 | 78 | ? |

○ 80   ○ 107   ○ 19   ○ 87   ○ 97

64 Tess is taller than Eddie, and Eddie is shorter than Rita. Which of the following must be true?

A Eddie is taller than Tess.

B Rita and Tess are both taller than Eddie.

C Eddie is taller than Rita.

D Rita is the tallest in the group.

E Rita is taller than Tess.

65 Lara has more stamps than Ella. Nat has more stamps than Julio. Olivia has fewer stamps than Ella but more stamps than Julio. Which of the following is true?

A Olivia has more stamps than Lara.

B Ella has more stamps than Lara.

C Nat has fewer stamps than Julio.

D Nat has more stamps than Lara.

E Julio has the fewest stamps.

66 Shaun is shorter than Maria. Landon is taller than Jess, but shorter than Shaun. Which of the following is true?

A Shaun is the tallest.

B Maria is shorter than Jess.

C Landon is shorter than Maria.

D Jess is taller than Shaun.

E Maria is the same height as Landon.

67 What number should replace the question mark (?) so that all three sets of numbers go together in the same way?

[3, 26]   [4, 63]   [5, ?]

124   125   126   127   128

68 What number should replace the question mark (?) so that all three sets of numbers go together in the same way?

[6, 25]   [8, 33]   [10, ?]

37   41   39   43   25

69 What number should replace the question mark (?) so that all three sets of numbers go together in the same way?

[4, 13]   [6, 33]   [8, ?]

61   62   63   64   65

70 Which choice makes the second set of pictures go together in the same way as the first set?

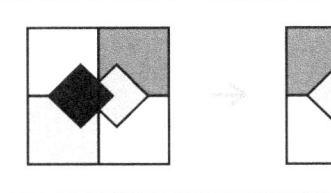
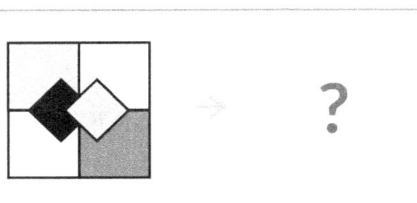

?

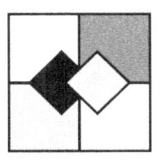
A

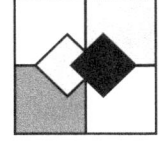
B

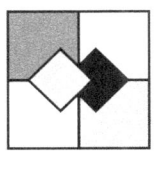
C

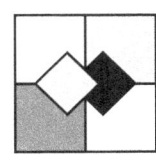
D

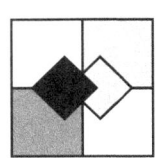
E

ANSWER KEY FOR PRACTICE TEST 1 (WORKBOOK FORMAT)

Antonyms

-1. D. Reject means to refuse or decline, while accept means to agree to or take in.
-2. C. Elevate means to lift or raise to a higher position, while lower means to bring down.
-3. A. Import means to bring in goods, while export means to send goods out.
-4. E. Reluctantly means with hesitation, while eagerly means with enthusiasm or readiness.

Sentence Completion

-5. B. asset = an advantage/a benefit
-6. C. optimal = best
-7. A. cultivate = to develop or improve with training
-8. B. scarcely = hardly/barely; harsh = very uncomfortable/unpleasant/stark

Sentence Arrangement

-9. B. Sentence: A positive attitude makes everything better.
-10. E. Sentence: The person who works hard succeeds.
-11. D. Sentence: I feel great and ready to start work.
-12. D. Sentence: I already had lunch with my friends.

Arithmetic Reasoning

-13. E. "Forty-five less than five times eighteen" means: $(5 \times 18) - 35$. $90 - 35 = 55$.
-14. A. When Noah finished, there were 5 minutes left: 25 minutes - 20 minutes = 5 minutes
-15. B. We add them all together: 30 minutes = 0.5 hours; $0.5 + 5.5 + 0.5 + 0.5 = 7$ hours
-16. B. $28 + 72 - 23$; $100 - 23 = 77$

Logical Selection

-17. C. A painting requires a surface, such as a canvas, a wall, or paper, on which paint is applied. Paintings do not always have frames, many colors (some paintings are a single color), signatures, or titles, especially in abstract or modern art.
-18. B. The defining feature of a shoe is the sole, which provides protection and support for the foot. Shoes do not always have laces (e.g., slip-ons), leather (e.g. shoes made out of another material), a brand logo (generic or handmade shoes may lack logos), or a tongue (sandals and some slip-ons don't have one).
-19. C. All pens must have ink to fulfill their purpose of writing or marking.
-20. D. Fabric is the essential material that makes up a shirt. Not all shirts have sleeves (e.g., tank tops), buttons (e.g., t-shirts), collars (e.g., casual shirts), or pockets.

Verbal Analogies

-21. A. Something heavy is defined by its great weight, like something fast is defined by its high speed.
-22. B. A theater is a place where movies are shown, like a museum is a place where artifacts are displayed/shown.
-23. C. A wagon was used in the past for transportation, like a car is used today, and a typewriter was used in the past for typing documents, like a computer is used today.
-24. D. A lung fills with air. Without air, the lung cannot serve its main function — breathing. An engine fills with fuel. Without fuel, the engine cannot serve its main function — powering the vehicle.

Verbal Classification

-25. B. verbs that mean "to stop"
-26. A. types of jobs that involve helping care for people
-27. E. different kinds of bags
-28. C. words that have to do with coming together for a common purpose or goal

Verbal Matrix

-29. E. Across the rows, use the first word, then take the vowel from the second word & put it after the vowel in the first word.
-30. C. Across the rows, the first letter stays the same, the vowel is doubled, and the second consonant is deleted.
-31. A. Down the columns, the words are in alphabetical order. In the third column, the top word begins with "T" (theory), so the missing word below it must begin with "U."
-32. D. In the first row, the word "stage" is a combination of "start" (the first 3 letters, "sta") and "gent" (the first 2 letters, "ge"). In the second row, combine the first three letters of "realm" ("rea") and the first two letters of "chat" ("ch") = "reach."

Inferences

-33. D. To solve this, let's create an ordered list based on the given information. We can summarize the sentences using "greater than" (>) and "less than" (<).
  -Tia runs faster than Joe: Tia > Joe
  -Joe runs slower than Sam but faster than Adam: Sam > Joe > Adam
This gives us the following possible order:
Tia > Sam > Joe > Adam   OR   Sam > Tia > Joe > Adam
In both possible scenarios, Adam is the slowest runner.
-34. E. Lee has fewer books than Olivia: Olivia > Lee
Olivia has more books than Ellie: Olivia > Ellie; So the order is: Olivia > Lee, Ellie
-35. A. We know this info: Alex is older than Ben. Alex > Ben
                            Chris is younger than Dev. Chris < Dev
                            Emily is older than Ben but younger than Chris: Ben < Emily < Chris
Combining the first and third statements: Ben < Emily < Chris < Dev
From this, we can conclude for certain that Ben is the youngest.

Figure Analogies

-36. A. bottom shape becomes top shape & gets smaller, middle shape becomes bottom shape & gets bigger, top shape becomes middle shape & gets bigger
-37. B. white circles become black stars; white trapezoids become gray parallelograms; black stars become white circles
-38. E. shapes "flip" to become a mirror image
-39. E. inside the square, the shape's number of sides increases by 1

Figure Series

-40. D. In each group, there are 3 arched shapes. In the first box, 2 arches point down & 1 arch points up. In each box, the arch that points up moves down 1 position. Also, the dotted line switches from the right side of the shape group to the left side of the shape group.
-41. A. 3 dotted triangles rotate clockwise around the shape group

ANSWER KEY FOR PRACTICE TEST 1 (WORKBOOK FORMAT), CONTINUED

Pattern Matrix

-42. D. in the second box, shapes flip in; in the third box the entire box then rotates 180°
-43. A. middle & last box have the same shapes from the first box
-44. D. gray rectangle moves clockwise once around group of circles

Numeric Matrix

-45. B. across rows: ÷7, ×4; down columns: ÷6, ×5
-46. A. across rows: ÷4, +5; down columns: same number that's added to the first number to get the second number is added again to get the third number (+4, +4 in first column; +1, +1 in second column; +1, +1 in second column)
-47. D. across rows: ÷5, ÷6; down columns: ÷2, ×3
-48. E. across rows: -8, -8; down columns: +3, -4

Numeric Inferences

-49. E. x4   -50. B. ×3, -3   -51. C. +31, x3   -52. B. x4, +8

Numeric Series

-53. B. numbers come in pairs where the second number is a "mirror" of the first number (the outer digits in the second number switch places); the first number in each pair is 4 less than the first number in the previous pair; the pattern is (mirror), -4, (mirror), -4, (mirror), etc.
-54. B. numbers come in pairs, where the second number is the mirror of the first number (the digits in the second number switch places); the first number in each pair is 6 more than the first number in the previous pair; the pattern is +6, (mirror), +6, (mirror), etc.
-55. C. every other number is 3 & in between the 3s, the series follows this rule: each number is greater than the previous number by 2
-56. C. each number is greater than the previous number by 2 more than the previous difference (starting with 6). The pattern is: +6, +8, +10, +12, ... 5 + 6, 11 + 8, 19 + 10, 29 + 12, 41 + 14, 55 + 16 = 71.

ANSWER KEY FOR PRACTICE TEST 2

- Note: At the end of each explanation is the OLSAT® question type in gray font (Antonyms, Sentence Arrangement, Arithmetic Reasoning, Figure Analogies, etc.).

-1. B. Include means to take in or involve, while exclude means to leave out or reject Antonyms
-2. B. Correct sentence: She will work at the brand new store. Sentence Arrangement
-3. A. Ten less than one-third of ninety is the same as (90 ÷ 3) - 10. 30 - 10 = 20. Arithmetic Reasoning
-4. C. group of triangles "flips"/is a mirror image (note that in the bottom box, when you flip the 2 triangles on the right, choice C is the only choice with the dark gray triangle & white triangles flipped correctly) Figure Analogies
-5. A. Stagnant means not moving or developing, while flowing means moving steadily or continuously. Antonyms
-6. C. A team cannot exist without people who are part of it. Teams do not necessarily need uniforms, a coach, a name, or equipment to be considered a team. Logical Selection
-7. D. the lowest part/deepest point of something Verbal Classification

-8. D. places used for storage that are enclosed Verbal Classification
-9. E. A fragment is a broken piece of metal, just as a crumb is a broken piece of bread. Verbal Analogies
-10. C. Correct sentence: The campers were almost bitten by a venomous snake. Sentence Arrangement
-11. B. Total number of packs: 3 + 2 + 4 = 9; 9 × 5 = 45 Arithmetic Reasoning
-12. B. upper left figure rotates 180° to face down; Upper right & lower right shapes switch and the new upper right becomes gray Figure Analogies
-13. B. across rows: -7, +9; down columns: -12 Numeric Matrix
-14. D. elated = feeling extremely happy or excited Sentence Completion
-15. A. Across, all three words begin with "r" in the first row & "m" in the second row. Going down the columns, in the first column the words end in -ock, in the second column, the words end in -iddle, in the third column, the words end in -ope. Verbal Matrix
-16. D. An artist is a type of occupation. A cathedral is a type of monument. Verbal Analogies
-17. C. significantly = to a notable or important degree Sentence Completion
-18. B: x2, ÷12 Numeric Inferences
-19. D. Correct sentence: Debris from the storm caused damage to several homes. Sentence Arrangement
-20. D. Five more than seven times seven is (7 x 7) + 5; 49 + 5 = 54 Arithmetic Reasoning
-21. A. A concert requires someone to create or present the music or performance. Not all concerts have tickets, a stage (e.g., street performances), an audience at all times (e.g., rehearsals or small events), or lights (e.g., daytime outdoor concerts). Logical Selection
-22. C. alphabetical order = organized by letter; chronological = organized by time Verbal Analogies
-23. E. large form > very small form Verbal Analogies
-24. A. Correct sentence: Anchors have chains that keep ships stable in the water. Sentence Arrangement
-25. D. Open space because parks are defined as areas with open space for recreation or relaxation. Not all parks have benches, trees (they could have other types of plants or none at all), walking paths, or water fountains. Logical Selection
-26. C. Something dense has a lot of mass. Something bright has a lot of light. Verbal Analogies
-27. B. object > object's top Verbal Analogies
-28. D. Across the rows, use the first word, then take the vowel from the second word & put it after the vowel in the first word. Verbal Matrix
-29. D. Acquire means to gain possession of something, while lose means to no longer have something. Antonyms
-30. E. depleted = depleted soil has lost its essential nutrients and minerals Sentence Completion
-31. E. 20 - 5 = 15 marbles; she loses 4, so 15 - 4 = 11 marbles; finally, she finds 3 marbles, so 11 + 3 = 14 marbles Arithmetic Reasoning
-32. A. A lens is needed because a camera cannot capture an image without one. Not all cameras have a tripod (which is optional for stability), film (e.g., digital cameras), or a flash (e.g., daytime or basic cameras). Logical Selection
-33. E: the pattern is: +1, +3, +5, +7, etc. Numeric Series
-34. D. Ambiguously means in a way that is unclear or can have more than one meaning, while clearly means in an easily understood and obvious way. Antonyms
-35. A. formidable = inspiring fear, dread, or apprehension; instruct = to give advice/share knowledge; to teach or train Sentence Completion
-36. C. verbs describing actions of standing still or staying in one place Verbal Classification

-37. E. verbs involved with moving/traveling from one place to another Verbal Classification

-38. D. synonyms Verbal Analogies

-39. B. -12, -10, -8, -6, -4, -2, etc. Numeric Series

-40. E. Across the rows, the first letter stays the same, the vowel is doubled, and the second consonant is deleted. Verbal Matrix

-41. E. in the second box, the shapes change to hexagons; note the original shapes are divided into quarters and the hexagons are divided into quarters; in the original shapes & in the hexagons, 1 quarter is black; this black quarter changes position from the original shape to the new hexagon like this: - bottom left in original shape > bottom right in hexagon
 - top left in original shape > bottom left in hexagon
 - bottom right in original shape > top left in hexagon
 - top right in original shape > top right in hexagon Figure Analogies

-42. D. An atom is a small part of a larger molecule, just as a verse is a small part of a larger poem. Verbal Analogies

-43. E. Each number is the sum of the previous two numbers.
$2 + 3 = 5; 3 + 5 = 8; 5 + 8 = 13; 8 + 13 = 21; 13 + 21 = 34$
To find the next number, we add the last two numbers: $21 + 34 = 55$. Numeric Series

-44. B. down the columns, the words are opposites Verbal Matrix

-45. C. top shape goes inside middle shape; top shape & middle shape get bigger; bottom shape becomes the center shape, rotates 90° counterclockwise, and turns gray Figure Analogies

-46. A. +345 Numeric Inferences

-47. C. the numbers come in pairs, where the first number is positive, and the second number is its negative counterpart; the next pair increases the absolute value by 2 Numeric Series

-48. C. across rows: +22; down columns: -13 Numeric Matrix

-49. B. The diagonal line dividing the shape switches from going upper left to lower right & lower left to upper right. Also, the design/color in the shape's half that faces the next shape is "mirrored" in the shape next to it. From box 1 to 2 it's wavy lines. From box 2 to 3 it's vertical lines. From 3 to 4 it's white. From 4 to 5 (the answer) it's wavy lines. Finally, in the other half of the shape (the half that does not have this "mirror" design), the design must be different than the shape that came before it. From box 1 to 2, it changes from white to vertical lines. From box 2 to 3, it changes from wavy lines to white. From box 3 to 4, it changes from vertical lines to wavy lines. From box 4 to 5, it changes from white to vertical lines. Figure Series

-50. E. across rows: +42, -53; down columns: -39, -45 Numeric Matrix

-51. A. Each box has one trapezoid filled with lines (the rest are white). In each box the shape filled with lines moves back one position (4-3-2-1). So, after it's in position 1, it must go back to 4. Figure Series

-52. C. across rows: -27 then +61; down columns: +34 then -29 Numeric Matrix

-53. B. 2 gray ovals move counterclockwise around the group of ovals Figure Series

-54. A. shape halves combine Pattern Matrix

-55. B. in each box, the number of gray sections increases by 1 & the gray sections are next to each other Figure Series

-56. C. across, shape rotates like this - second box: 180°, third box: 90° clockwise Pattern Matrix

-57. C. each row & column must have a one of each shape (thin black hexagon, gray square, thin hexagon with dots); each row & column must also have one of each quantity of wavy lines (1 line, 2 lines or 3 lines) and they must be going the same direction Pattern Matrix

-58. C. In every box, the crescent moves clockwise around the grid. As it moves, it switches pointing up to pointing down. In *every other* box, the trapezoid moves clockwise. Figure Series

-59. D. +15, -16 Numeric Inferences

-60. D. one box of each row/column is a combo of the other two boxes Pattern Matrix

-61. D.

1. note the design of each line: dashed, black, wavy, or gray
2. dashed line rule: each box has a dashed line & this dashed line must be in a different position across each row & down each column the dashed line must be in a different position
3. rules for lines that are either black, wavy, or gray (not dashed lines):
-in each row/column, each line type (black, wavy, or gray) will only be in 2 out of the 3 boxes in each row/column
-in the rows, these lines (black, wavy, or gray) will be in a different position
-in the columns, however, these lines (black, wavy, or gray) will be in the same position
Pattern Matrix

-62. C. ×7, -33 Numeric Inferences

-63. D. We can summarize the sentences. Elisa > Daniel -and- Sophia > Rachel -and-
Rachel < Olivia < Daniel; So, we can conclude that Daniel has more books than Rachel. Inferences

-64. A. Sarah > Tom -and- Maria > Lily > James -and- Lily > Sarah > James
Combining the second and third statements, we get: Maria > Lily > Sarah > James
Therefore, we can conclude that: A. Maria has the highest grade. Inferences

-65. D. upper left figure rotates 180° to face down; upper right & lower right shapes switch and the new upper right becomes gray Figure Analogies

-66. A. +1, +1, +2; +1, +1, +2, etc. Numeric Series

-67. C. ×2, +1, ×2, +1, etc. Numeric Series

-68. E. ×4, ÷2, ×4, ÷2 Numeric Series

-69. E. synonyms Verbal Analogies

-70. C. Negligence may cause an accident as a disease may cause an epidemic. Verbal Analogies

ANSWER KEY FOR PRACTICE TEST 3

-1. C. Exhaust means to use up or tire out, while replenish means to refill or restore. Antonyms

-2. D. Olivia starts with $50. She spends $25 on a shirt: $50 - $25 = $25.
Then she spends $8 on flip-flops: $25 - $8 = $17. Finally, she spends $10 on a hat:
$17 - $10 = $7. Arithmetic Reasoning

-3. C. numbers decrease by 3, 4, 5, 6, 7, 8, 9, etc. Numeric Series

-4. C. x6, x6 Numeric Inferences

-5. A. Productive means producing results or being effective, while idle means inactive or not working. Antonyms

-6. B. Four more than the square root of sixteen is the same as $4 + \sqrt{16}$. This is 4 + 4 = 8.
Arithmetic Reasoning

-7. B. ×1, ×1, ÷1; ×2, ×2, ÷2; ×3, ×3, ÷3 Numeric Series

-8. A. +93 Numeric Inferences

-9. E. Compassionate means showing kindness and concern, while unkind means not kind.
Antonyms

-10. A. on top, dark gray rectangle with 1/4 filled w/ diagonal lines becomes a circle filled with dots and the same amount (1/4) filled with diagonal lines; on the bottom, the dotted rectangle with 1/2 filled w/ diagonal lines becomes dark gray circle with same amount (1/2) filled with dark gray; note that the design & quantity of the inside lines must be the same also Figure Analogies

-11. C. -84 Numeric Inferences

-12. D. across rows, the number in the 2nd column is subtracted from number in 1st column to number in 3rd column (1st-2nd=3rd); down columns, the 2nd number is the sum of 1st and 3rd numbers (1st+3rd=2nd) Numeric Matrix

-13. C. Converge means to come together from different directions, while separate means to move apart or divide. Antonyms

-14. D. shape group becomes a "mirror image," then the hexagon moves in front of the diamond and becomes filled with dots; diamond changes from dark gray to light gray; large square changes from light gray to dark gray Figure Analogies

-15. D. the third number is the sum of the first and second number Numeric Inferences

-16. B. every other number, starting with -3, is 3x the previous; every other number, starting with -7, increases by 9 Numeric Series

-17. A. Sentence: Trees have roots that keep them anchored in the soil. Sentence Arrangement

-18. B. Rooms are essential because a hotel must provide rooms for guests to stay in. Not all hotels have a swimming pool, a restaurant, a concierge, or wi-fi. Logical Selection

-19. A. Across the rows, take the first 2 letters from the first word & add them to the second word. (st + rain = strain; sl + ant = slant) Verbal Matrix

-20. D. x8 Numeric Inferences

-21. E. Correct sentence: Glasses have frames that keep the lenses in place. Sentence Arrangement

-22. C. precise = exact and accurate in measurement or description Sentence Completion

-23. C. A bank's primary purpose is to store and manage money. Not all banks have tellers (for example, online-only banks), vaults, ATMs, or checks. Logical Selection

-24. E. -281, ÷3 Numeric Inferences

-25. D. Sentence: The exhausted hikers avoided an attack by a ferocious bear. Sentence Arrangement

-26. E. pristine = something that is in its original, pure, or unspoiled condition Sentence Completion

-27. C. to the third power Numeric Inferences

-28. D. Airports require runways for airplanes to take off and land. Not all airports have baggage claim areas (e.g., small airports), security checkpoints (e.g., private airports), control towers (e.g., small airstrips), or restaurants. Logical Selection

-29. E. -1, +2, -3 | -4, +5, -6 | -7 , +8, -9 Numeric Series

-30. D. Rain from a storm enabled plants to grow. Sentence Arrangement

-31. D. strenuous = demanding, requiring a lot of effort; altitudes = heights above sea level Sentence Completion

-32. B. divide by 4, then -3 Arithmetic Reasoning

-33. C. Not all plants have:
-flowers: Many plants, like mosses and ferns, do not produce flowers.
-leaves: Some plants, like cacti, do not have leaves.
-stems: Plants like moss do not have stems.
-soil: Plants like orchids grow without soil.
Plant cells, however, are universal to all plants and are essential for their growth and survival. Logical Selection

-34. B. ×1, ×1, ÷1; ×2, ×2, ÷2; ×3, ×3, ÷3 Numeric Series

-35. B. An editor's role is to revise, just as a translator's role is to interpret. Verbal Analogies

-36. D. A chisel is a tool used in sculpture. A scalpel is a tool used in surgery. Verbal Analogies

-37. E. having to do with 3 Verbal Classification

-38. A. different parts of a book's content (an author writes books but is not a specific part of a book's content) Verbal Classification
-39. E. across the rows, take the 2 letters in the second column & put them in front of the 2 letters in the first column Verbal Matrix
-40. A. An innovative person has a lot of creativity, just as a resolute person has a lot of determination. Verbal Analogies
-41. C. If something is infallible, it has no error. If something is immutable, it has no change. Verbal Analogies
-42. D. related to copying or reproducing something Verbal Classification
-43. D. related to continuing or keeping something going Verbal Classification
-44. B. Here, it helps to look at the last word in the first row & then work backwards. Assign numbers (1,2,3,4) to each letter of the last word. The last word in the first row is "EDIT."
So, E=1, D=2, I=3; T=4. Then, take these letter/number assignments and apply them to the first two sets of letters in the first row. Doing this, the formula is: 14 + 23 = 1234; ET + DI = EDIT
In the bottom row, use this formula again, 14 + 23 = 1234; T=1, M=4; E=2, A=3.
Therefore, TEAM is the answer. Verbal Matrix
-45. B. across the first row, take the first three letters of "desert" ("des") and the last three letters of the second word "align" ("ign"); in the second row do the same: combine the first three letters of "shade" ("sha") and the last three letters of the second word "mopes" ("pes") = "shapes"
Verbal Matrix
-46. A. shape rotates 180° & wavy lines become light gray Figure Analogies
-47. A. squared Numeric Inferences
-48. B. every other number, starting with -3, is 3x the previous; every other number, starting with 0, increases by 3. Numeric Series
-49. B. down columns, the 2 words are opposites Verbal Matrix
-50. E. order of shapes reverses -and- the 2nd shape & the 4th shape turn gray Figure Analogies
-51. A. to the third power, then +2 Numeric Inferences
-52. C. across rows: number in 1st column is multiplied by 5 to get number in 2nd column; then the number in 1st column is multiplied by 4 to get the number in 3rd column ((1st) × 5, (1st) × 4); down the columns, 3rd number is the sum of 1st and 2nd numbers (1st + 2nd = 3rd)
Numeric Matrix
-53. E. "L" becomes "I"; equal sign becomes plus; "I" becomes "L"; equal sign becomes plus sign Figure Analogies
-54. D. across rows, the number in 3rd column is the sum of the numbers in the 1st and 2nd columns (1st+2nd=3rd); down columns, ÷6 Numeric Matrix
-55. E. across rows: ×2, ÷4; down columns: ×8, ÷5 Numeric Matrix
-56. B. gray sections combine in the last box Pattern Matrix
-57. D. in each box, the group of 2 arrows rotates 90 degrees clockwise Figure Series
-58. D. first, note the design of each oval: dotted, black, white, or gray;
-dotted oval rule: each box has an oval filled with dots & this dotted oval must be in a different spot across each row & down each column
-color oval rule #1: for the ovals filled with black, white, or gray, in each row/column, each color oval will only be in 2 out of the 3 boxes in the row/column
-color oval rule #2: in the rows, each color oval (black, white, or gray) will be in a different spot
-color oval rule #3: in the columns, each color oval will be in the same spot Pattern Matrix
-59. A. across each row, the triangle & heart move counterclockwise inside the grid's sections; the final box in the row continues that pattern Pattern Matrix
-60. C. multiply by 3 Numeric Series

-61. D. across rows/down columns, there are 3 different shapes & each of those must be in 3 different positions across the rows/down the columns -and- the upper left position must be empty Pattern Matrix

-62. D. in top set, octagon switches from gray to wavy lines; lower left circle changes to a triangle, moves to the upper right, and the design inside changes from wavy lines to gray; in the bottom, it's the reverse: octagon changes from filled with wavy lines to gray, circle changes to a triangle & changes its position and design (gray to wavy); no change with rectangle Figure Analogies

-63. E. add 19 Numeric Series

-64. B. Tess is taller than Eddie: Tess > Eddie; Eddie is shorter than Rita: Rita > Eddie

From this, we know that Rita and Tess are both taller than Eddie. Inferences

-65. E. Lara has more stamps than Ella: Lara > Ella

Nat has more stamps than Julio: Nat > Julio

Olivia has fewer stamps than Ella but more stamps than James: Ella > Olivia > Julio

Now, Lara > Ella > Olivia > Julio -and- Nat > Julio

From this, we can conclude that Julio has the fewest stamps. Inferences

-66. C. Shaun is shorter than Maria: Maria > Shaun

Landon is taller than Jess, but shorter than Shaun: Shaun > Landon > Jess

When you combine the two: Maria > Shaun > Landon > Jess; So, Landon is shorter than Maria.
Inferences

-67. A. raise to third power, then -1 Numeric Analogies

-68. B. x4, then +1 Numeric Analogies

-69. A. squared, then -3 Numeric Analogies

-70. D. mirror image of original figure Figure Analogies